RALLY POINT

RALLY POINT

Five Tasks to Unite the Country and
Revitalize the American Dream

CHRIS GIBSON

TWELVE

New York Boston

Twelve
Hachette Book Group
1290 Avenue of the Americas, New York, NY 10104
twelvebooks.com
twitter.com/twelvebooks

First Edition: October 2017

Twelve is an imprint of Grand Central Publishing. The Twelve name and logo are trademarks of Hachette Book Group, Inc.

Unless otherwise noted, photos courtesy of Chris Gibson.

The publisher is not responsible for websites (or their content) that are not owned by the publisher.

The Hachette Speakers Bureau provides a wide range of authors for speaking events. To find out more, go to www.hachettespeakersbureau.com or call (866) 376-6591.

Library of Congress Cataloging-in-Publication Data has been applied for.

ISBNs: 978-1-5387-6058-1 (hardcover), 978-1-5387-6057-4 (ebook)

Printed in the United States of America

LSC-C

10 9 8 7 6 5 4 3 2 1

For the brave men and women who defend us and protect our exceptional way of life

In Memory of Staff Sergeant Zachary Wobler and Sergeant Chris Pusateri
Killed in Action in Iraq, February 2005

Contents

rally point—

1. An easily identifiable point on the ground at which units can reassemble and reorganize if they become dispersed;

2. An easily identifiable point on the ground at which aircrews and passengers can assemble and reorganize following an incident requiring a forced landing.

Army Field Manual 1-02 Operational
Terms and Graphics

Introduction

Gibson in Baghdad, Iraq, serving as Commander of the 2nd Battalion, 325th Airborne, in December 2004.

For the majority of Americans, the 2016 presidential campaign was not a positive experience. Both major candidates were deeply unpopular, with unfavorable ratings well above 50 percent. That is unprecedented in American politics. Donald Trump and Hillary Clinton were widely viewed as divisive and dismissive of large swaths of the electorate. Given the results of this election, Americans are deeply divided and uncertain about the direction of the country and wonder whether we can come together to tackle our significant challenges.

Donald Trump won the presidency, and for conservatives that presents opportunities and challenges. First, however, we must recognize this stark reality: We are not only a nation divided—as Republicans we are also a party divided. I am not interested in pointing fingers and assigning blame. The purpose of this book is to unify and grow our conservative ranks so that we rally the nation around our principles, consistently win elections, and earn the trust of the American people to stay the course with our solutions.

The United States was an exceptional nation at birth, different from the rest of the world because we believed in God-given natural rights and were bold enough to establish a government that protected those rights with the citizen in charge. Today we are still that exceptional nation, and I am confident that if we find our voice and rally the American people, we will bring forward the solutions required to restore the American dream and revitalize our republic. The key is focus, and for that we need leadership.

As conservatives, we must lay out a positive vision for America. That plan must accomplish five essential tasks:

- *Strengthen our national security*
- *Restore founding principles*
- *Promote a flourishing life*
- *Keep faith*
- *Unify and grow the movement*

Over the next five chapters, I address those challenges. In chapter one, I make the case for a "peace through strength" grand strategy that restores deterrence, defeats terrorists, and advances U.S. interests through diplomacy and a thriving economy. In chapter two, I define the "Spirit of Philadelphia" demonstrating how that founding and its covenants and compromises helped facilitate peace and prosperity at home and eventually elevated us to a world superpower. I also show how deviating from founding principles over time caused significant challenges and national disunity, before concluding with recommendations for revitalizing our democracy. In chapter three, I lay out a plan to unleash economic growth so that all Americans can enjoy the American Dream. In chapter four, I explain why keeping faith in God, ourselves, our family, friends, and community is so central to a flourishing American future. Chapter five provides a political blueprint for unifying and growing the conservative movement so that we can rally and lift up the country. I conclude the book with analysis of the 2016 presidential election, President Trump, and the future of the GOP, invoking our first Republican president, Abraham Lincoln, to tackle the formidable challenges ahead.

We are all products of our experiences. I am no different. This book reflects over fifty years of experience from the "School of Hard Knocks." I grew up in a working-class family in upstate New York, the oldest of a family of four children raised in the Irish Catholic tradition. Not surprisingly given our background, my parents were Demo crats. All of our family had been Democrats since arriving from the old country—I was the first Republican, for reasons I will explain later.

I enlisted as a private in the infantry of the New York Army National Guard in 1981 at the age of seventeen, motivated to protect and defend this cherished way of life. I made the transition from enlisted man to officer through the ROTC program at nearby Siena College (a small Catholic college), and went on to serve twenty-four more years in the regular Army. Like nearly everyone in the military over that period, I served multiple combat tours (four to be exact) in the Middle East, a NATO peace enforcement deployment in the Balkans, a humanitarian relief operation in Haiti, and a counter-drug operation in the southwestern United States.

Two great Americans, battle-hardened paratroopers Sergeant Chris Pusateri and Staff Sergeant Zachary Wobler, were killed in Iraq while serving under my command in the 82nd Airborne Division. I will tell their story of courage and sacrifice in these pages.

Dozens more were wounded in action, including some grievously. I was wounded myself (fortunately not seriously) while leading these brave paratroopers. Like our brothers and sisters before us in previous wars, none of us who served over there came home the same person. We were fundamentally changed by these experiences. Our country is still coming to grips with this reality in the midst of extensive efforts to help our veterans make the transition.

In some ways, my military experience reinforced who I was from childhood. I am deeply spiritual and reflective. I believe fervently in American exceptionalism, and I remain grateful— thankful that I was born American. I feel as if I won the lottery, by birthright a recipient of the American dream. I have lived that dream.

My combat experience also informed, and significantly influenced, my actions for six years as a member of the U.S. House of Representatives. Throughout that time I was a committed and passionate voice for reform. I am not wearing rose-tinted glasses. I see the problems that exist in our country today. As a U.S. representative, I listened carefully to my constituents. I understand their concerns and know their deep desire for change. Many Americans feel that our political system is rigged for moneyed interests and those with political connections to the nation's elite. Ordinary American citizens believe this system no longer works for them. *They are right.* It is past time to "drain the swamp."

We must fight for change that restores founding principles and promotes a flourishing life for all Americans. I've written this book to help in that cause, explaining how we can promote and secure liberty and reform the economy so that it works for everyone, including working-class families like the one I grew up in.

Influenced by the Founders, I'm a strong believer in a government "of the people, by the people, for the people." We were never intended to have a permanent political class. Accordingly, I self-imposed term limits and recently completed my time in Congress. Still, I remain passionate about our nation and want to help us find our voice to rally this great nation so that the twenty-first century is our best century yet. Toward that end, I appreciate your willingness to read this book and hope that you will keep faith in our exceptional way of life and join me in fighting for this worthy cause.

Chris Gibson
Kinderhook, New York
June 1, 2017

CHAPTER 1

Practice Peace through Strength

The High Personal Cost of Freedom

In many ways, Army sergeant Chris Pusateri was a typical para-trooper. An adventurous, avid outdoorsman from upstate New York, Chris exuded confidence, competence, and enjoyed life. He was a good soldier.

As a battalion commander in the 82nd Airborne Division, I had approximately nine hundred of these dedicated Americans orga-nized under my charge in Iraq. I became acquainted with Chris in the fall of 2004 as our battalion was intensively training for possible deployment to Iraq when we assumed Division Ready Force (DRF) status around Thanksgiving. Chris walked up to me in the chow hall one day to ask about my earlier experiences in the 10th Moun-tain Division, a unit stationed at Fort Drum near Watertown, New York, approximately three hours from Chris's hometown of Painted Post. Chris was interested in being posted closer to home where he could hunt and fish with his high school buddies on weekends. He knew that I had served with the 10th Mountain Division from 2000 to 2002 and wanted my advice on whether he should reenlist in the Army after his initial term ended in less than a year.

I was struck by the careful manner in which Pusateri approached me. Like all Army units, the 82nd Airborne Division placed command emphasis and great pride in seeing their soldiers reenlist for "present duty station." Indeed, "Stay 82nd" paraphernalia (shirts, fleeces, pens, notebooks, and so on) was replete in all local reenlistment offices up and down Ardennes Street at Fort Bragg, North Carolina, where battalions of that storied unit maintain barracks to this day. The intent was clear—persuade paratroopers to remain in the division.

Chris was no doubt aware of that pressure. After he broached the topic of a possible reenlistment option of assignment at Fort Drum, he quickly stated, "Is that disloyal, sir?" I assured him it was not. While I certainly welcomed his reenlistment with our unit, for the bigger picture of an Army at war, what was most important was that we kept him in boots. I then told him about the 10th Mountain Division—it was a tremendous place to serve. Living in the "North Country" of upstate New York was also an immensely enjoyable experience for a person raised in that state, and an experience we shared. Shortly after that, Pusateri reenlisted for Fort Drum and the Army put in motion the orders that would return him to New York early in the coming year.

That was early November 2004. Things change rapidly in the 82nd Airborne Division. Right after Thanksgiving, our battalion was alerted for immediate deployment to Iraq to reinforce "Route Irish," the highway between the Baghdad airport and the Green Zone, the center of government. That area was the scene of dozens of insurgent vehicle-borne improvised explosive device (VBIED) attacks. Senior military leaders in Iraq, including the local brigade commander, Colonel Mark Milley (now General Milley, the chief of staff of the Army), and at the Pentagon were intent on defeating these deadly insurgent cells so that the first-ever free elections in Iraq could be conducted safely at the end of January.

Within twenty-four hours of alert notification, our first element was en route to Iraq. The outload of the Division Ready Force can be a very challenging and stressful experience. The logistics plan is ambitious, with little margin for delay or error. As boxes and pallets are prepared and sent to the airfield for overseas movement, paratroopers go through final medical and personnel screening (updating shots and legal documents as necessary), and leaders begin an intensive planning phase for operations. It is a hectic environment to say the least. In that frenzy, I received word through Pusateri's company commander, Captain Joe Blanton, and First Sergeant Greg Nowak that Chris wanted to tear up his reenlistment contract so he could deploy to Iraq with his fellow paratroopers. He did not think it was right for his friends to go forward into combat while he stayed behind so he could transfer stations to Fort Drum.

This was a serious request. As busy as we were, it was important to get that decision right. I asked my command sergeant major, Richard Flowers, a charismatic leader from Brooklyn, New York, to assemble the entire chain of command, including Pusateri, so that we could talk directly with him and hear from his frontline supervisors. Two hours later we assembled in my office. Pusateri once again impressed me. He communicated very clearly, respectfully, and decisively that it was his strongest desire to deploy with us, and that he wanted his reenlistment papers torn up or deferred. His chain of command was unanimous in support. I approved the action. It was done—Pusateri would deploy with us, and upon our return he would report to Fort Drum.

"Pusa," as he was affectionately known to his fellow paratroopers of Delta Company, was always there for his buddies, and his last day on earth was no different. It was February 16, 2005, and we were in Mosul, northern Iraq. After serving for about a month securing Route Irish in Baghdad, we had been sent with no notice to reinforce Mosul after the deadly mess hall bombing there just before Christmas. Throughout our time there, our battalion was in constant combat with determined insurgent cells.

In the early morning hours of that fated day, Sergeant Pusateri finished an all-night shift standing security watch on the third floor of a three-story building on the eastern side of the Tigris River and at about 6:00 a.m. was settling in with his sleeping bag for some much-needed rest. At roughly 6:30 a.m., a major gunfight broke out. At that point, Chris could have stayed in his sleeping bag, because we had enough firepower at the site to defeat the enemy attack. Paratroopers, however, are known for their initiative, and instead, Sergeant Pusateri sprang into action, putting on his battle gear and moving to a position on the roof to help secure the flank of one of his buddies. During this gunfight, the enemy was firing an RPK machine gun with armor-piercing incendiary rounds, and they penetrated the concrete wall protecting Pusateri. One round hit the butt of his rifle and ricocheted, making contact with Pusateri's jaw before moving to the back of his skull.

We did everything we could. Chris was treated by our medics and quickly moved to the Mosul Field Hospital, where he was stabilized and prepared for helicopter transport to Balad—the highest level of medical care in theater. We needed to move him there because unless he could undergo an advanced medical procedure to temporarily remove part of his skull to allow room for the brain to swell and then naturally retract after treatment and time, he could not survive. Our medical professionals swiftly stabilized Chris and he was placed on the helicopter.

Tragically, Pusateri died of his wounds while in the air.

The next day, as I prepared for his memorial ceremony, I learned that Sergeant Chris Pusateri had been born on the Fourth of July (1983). That struck me as apt—*he was red, white, and blue to the core.*

Where do we find soldiers like these?

Staff Sergeant Zachary Wobler was a natural leader, well known and admired throughout our battalion. Deadly accurate with a rifle, he may have been our best sniper. Among his many talents, he was also a gifted guitar player and wrote interesting, funny (and sometimes colorful) songs, which our paratroopers loved. His wit was as lethal as his marksmanship—no one in the chain of command was safe from his hijinks and irreverent limericks.

Born in Snowflake, Virginia, before moving with his father to Ohio for high school, Zach possessed a strong intellect. I'm convinced he could have attended one of our nation's best colleges. He chose to enlist in the Army instead. In 2002, he was chosen over more than fifteen thousand talented others as the 82nd Airborne Division's "Paratrooper of the Year." At the ceremony in his honor, when he was interviewed by the local paper, the *Fayetteville Observer*, about this high achievement, Zach credited his father, who Wobler said "was big on honesty. That's one thing that was drilled into our family when I was young." When asked about the ongoing war and his thoughts on potential deployment, Wobler stated that "nobody knows 'til it comes down to it whether you are ready or not." The next February he found out. He deployed and took part in the invasion of Iraq in March 2003. His performance was exemplary. He rose quickly within the ranks. During our deployment for Operation Iraqi Freedom II, he was already a staff sergeant and held the important responsibilities of scout sniper team leader attached to our Charlie Company.

Through the hard work of Wobler and all of our paratroopers, Mosul stabilized and the election came off safely. The city's residents turned out in large numbers to participate in their future. Watching the Iraqis stand up to Al Qaeda was a powerfully emotional experience. Al Qaeda had threatened to kill those who voted. The Iraqi people are proud and courageous, and that threat inspired many to vote who might not have otherwise participated. To reduce potential voter fraud, the Iraqi government decided to have all voters dip a finger in purple ink after voting so that individuals would be deterred from trying to vote twice. Little did they know that this requirement would provide the opportunity for Iraqis to visibly spurn Al Qaeda, proudly displaying their colorful, visible sign for democratic participation at post-election rallies and photo opportunities. It gave new meaning to giving terrorists the finger.

Shortly thereafter, our brigade commander, Colonel (now four-star general) Bob Brown repositioned our battalion to help set the conditions of success for the newly elected Iraqi government preparing to take charge. Mosul's streets were still very dangerous, and at six foot five, Brown was a towering presence who inspired them in a way that reminded me of President Lincoln, who at six-four also stood out as he walked unsafe streets during the Civil War. Brown was a former Army basketball player under legendary Duke coach Mike Krzyzewski, a West Point graduate himself who in the late 1970s managed the West Point squad. Brown maintained his relationship with Coach K over the years, and that Christmas, Krzyzewski sent more than five thousand care packages to Mosul for all of his former player's soldiers. Sometimes it's the little things in life that make a big difference. That gesture engendered tremendous goodwill and lifted all of our spirits during a difficult time. Meanwhile, the enemy, still reeling from our victory over them in January's battles, continued to aggressively attack in an effort to regain the initiative. These actions took a toll on us, including on February 6, 2005, the day we lost Staff Sergeant Zachary Wobler.

That day began well. Wobler's sniper team, from a covered and concealed overwatch position they had established the previous night, surprised a pair of insurgents attempting to emplace improvised explosive devices (IEDs) on one of the main roads in east Mosul. Wobler and his team shot them both at a distance of about two hundred meters, immediately killing one and wounding the second.

According to the protocols of the Geneva Convention and the Law of Land Warfare, once an enemy soldier is incapacitated from wounds, he is no longer a combatant, and, seeing the wounded enemy crawling on the ground, Wobler's team moved from their positions toward the insurgent. When they got to him, it was clear he was badly wounded. They moved him off the road to an alley for treatment. At that point, a vehicle containing what we believe was the IED team's security force drove by at a high rate of speed down the road. When they were perpendicular with the alley where Wobler and his team were performing first aid on the wounded enemy soldier, two insurgents inside the vehicle delivered a burst of AK-47 rounds. One of those rounds hit Staff Sergeant Wobler in the side (missing both the front and back body armor plates that could have saved his life), severely damaging internal organs. As his paratrooper buddies began to perform first aid on him, Wobler insisted he not be evacuated. He wanted to remain on the battlefield leading his paratroopers. Despite his protestations, the Charlie Company first sergeant quickly overruled him and ordered his immediate evacuation to the Mosul Field Hospital. The doctors there did all they could for Wobler, but in the end he died of his wounds.

In the attempt to save the life of an enemy soldier, Staff Sergeant Zachary Wobler lost his own. Like those of Pusateri, Wobler's actions were courageous and selfless. It is important to tell their stories so that all Americans can appreciate their sacrifices.

In the days that followed, our battalion was able to kill the insurgents who took Wobler's and Pusateri's lives. Through a series of effective counterinsurgent operations in February and March 2005, we destroyed that enemy cell and stabilized our zone of Mosul. It came at a high price—our battalion had two killed in action (Pusateri and Wobler) and thirty-one wounded in action.

I will never forget those days in Iraq. Whenever I hear someone say, "Freedom isn't free," I think of Pusateri and Wobler. These young men lived their lives with integrity, dedicated to a cause greater than themselves. In their loss, they left holes in their families that will never be filled. Wobler left behind a beautiful baby girl, Trinity—barely three years old when her father was killed in action. In 2017, she will be fifteen years old, but her dad will not get to see her attend the high school prom, will not get the opportunity to walk her down the aisle someday.

Over time, I got to know Zach's mom, Jeanette Poston, and stepdad, Tim, as they were gracious enough to attend our memorial ceremonies and 82nd Airborne Division reunion events held annually during the last week of May. I first met them the day we got back from Iraq, although I was unaware that they had traveled to Fort Bragg to greet us. An amazing, selfless couple, they thought it was important to be there to welcome home all of Zach's buddies returning from war.

I had just dismissed the formation so that my paratroopers and I could enjoy the reunion celebration among our family and friends when Jeanette walked up. I was surprised and speechless, unable to find the right words to express my sorrow. I just hugged her while we both teared up. I was struck by her generosity and remarkable courage. She had lost her son to this war such a short time before, and now she was standing there among all the families to welcome the rest of us home. She could tell how badly I felt and sensed my awkwardness, reaching for my hand to reassure me. That kindness in the face of such personal sorrow was unbelievable. I wondered if I could do the same confronted with that tragedy. In that moment, I learned from Jeanette a lifetime's worth of grace and magnanimity. I've periodically stayed in touch with the Postons over the years and have greatly appreciated their encouragement for my congressional service. They are strong patriots who fiercely believe in this cherished way of life.

Similarly, I remember one of Pusateri's family members, a very young boy about seven years old, crying at the memorial ceremony we had for both of our fallen heroes at the Airborne and Special Operations Museum in Fayetteville, North Carolina, later in the summer of 2005. It was a surreal experience—an entire formation of hardened paratroopers standing at rigid attention as we honored Pusateri, and when this boy cried, there seemed like nothing in the world that could fix that or even make it better for him. Pusateri's widow, Christine, only nineteen years old, was understandably overwhelmed by the whole ordeal.

Sometimes fate works in ways beyond our comprehension. The Pusateris' family dog had just given birth to several very excitable young pups craving attention. This proved especially challenging for Christine. My wife, Mary Jo, and our executive officer Major Peter Wilhelm's wife, Erica, stepped in to help. We each adopted one of those puppies. Today, we still have Falcon (we called him that in honor of our brigade, which carries "Falcon" as its nickname), and every time I look at him, I'm reminded of Chris and the heavy price of freedom.

In the summer of 2016, I had the opportunity to visit Pusateri's grave. Many emotions came flooding back while I was kneeling at the gravesite. I reflected on all that had changed since the fateful day in February 2005, and wondered where Pusateri would have been today if he were still alive. Ultimately, I couldn't escape the painful sadness. Before I departed, I left one of my congressional coins on Chris's headstone. Shortly thereafter, his widow, Christine, posted on my congressional Facebook page expressing gratitude for the coin. I sent a private message in response and we subsequently had a nice phone conversation. It was great to be back in contact and to learn she was well. I stayed in touch with Chris's mom, Brenda West, for a number of years too, including exchanging emails on the anniversary of losing Chris. I always appreciated her strength and stoicism. We must always remember these heroes and honor their families' sacrifices on behalf of all of us.

I share these stories for two reasons. First, to personalize the stark reality that there is a high cost associated with the use of force. Accordingly, it is paramount that policymakers know what they are doing. These decisions require careful examination and consideration. It is wrong when political leaders make glib statements about impending military operations without really understanding the nature of warfare and the consequences of their words. War is always hard. It is sometimes necessary but should always be a last resort. Political leaders need to listen carefully to those with experience. Military leaders owe their civilian bosses candid assessments—information, analysis, and advice. Policymakers ignore their input at peril. The lives of Americans like Pusateri and Wobler, and countless others, are on the line. We must get these decisions right.

The second reason I share these stories is to communicate how these heartbreaking experiences have affected me. My duty in Iraq has changed me in many ways, both personally and professionally. I am more in touch with my emotions. I am more present in the moment and strengthened in my faith. I am also more methodical in my personal decision making. Professionally, I am more tempered in my views regarding the use of military force.

The Social Contract

To be clear, these experiences did not make me a pacifist. We must defend our freedom. I am a realist, grounded with a deep appreciation for history, which informs me that the best way to keep the peace while preserving our liberty is to deter potential adversaries with strong military preparation. As English philosopher Edmund Burke once stated, "The only thing necessary for the triumph of evil in the world is for good men to do nothing."

Society forms to provide for security. Enlightenment philosophers Thomas Hobbes, Jean-Jacques Rousseau, and John Locke all waxed eloquent on the "social contract," stating that the reason man leaves the state of nature and volitionally enters into civil society is to reduce vulnerability. There also is safety in numbers. The more individuals who join a security arrangement, the more formidable the alliance appears, potentially deterring attacks from other groups. Logically, this is the basis for forming government—to establish a security arrangement that protects those joining from the specter of a violent death.

The Declaration of Independence is our social contract. In it our Founders boldly asserted that as humans we have God-given natural rights. Governments are created by men to secure these rights, deriving their just powers from the consent of the governed. From this it is clear—*the first function of government is to protect its people and their rights.*

The Founders believed we could achieve security through deterrence. One of our earliest mottos was "Don't tread on me." What was implied was, "If you don't tread on us, we won't tread on you." In his farewell address, President George Washington reinforced that approach, warning against foreign entanglements that could drag us into unnecessary wars. Geography helped. The two large oceans between us and Europe and Asia kept us out of wars on those continents in the nineteenth century, and once Great Britain became an ally after the Treaty of Ghent, their superior navy augmented ours and significantly strengthened U.S. deterrence. For most of our history, "peace through strength" has been an effective approach for American national security.

In recent years, however, we have departed from this approach and have been too quick to use military force. The influence of "neoconservative" thinking favoring preemptive use of force has led to mistakes in places like Iraq and Libya. We must learn from these experiences and return to founding principles.

Thus our first task is to return to "peace through strength." We must move away from neoconservative foreign policy approaches. I have a theory about such things. Anytime you have to put a prefix (like "neo-") in front of a word to describe a thing, it's no longer that original thing. In fact, "neoconservative" foreign policy is not conservative at all. This philosophical approach, advanced by both the George W. Bush and Obama administrations, militarizes foreign policy and squanders, not conserves, precious resources. Bush invaded Iraq and Obama attacked Libya. Both of these were wars of choice, pursuing foreign regime change without provocation. That is not the American way. The consequences have been staggering in American lives and financial cost. We're now $20 trillion in debt, which threatens the republic, and we have a generation of veterans with physical and mental health issues who will need our support for the next fifty years. After all this, we are not much safer, if at all. Additionally, after more than fifteen years of persistent combat, our military is now worn out and must be reconstituted to restore deterrence. In some ways, our current situation is similar to 1979, when U.S. deterrence was weakened by lower readiness levels before President Reagan revitalized the military.

Reagan the Disrupter

President Reagan campaigned for the highest office in our land as a critic of the prevailing wisdom of that day—the bipartisan consensus for "détente." Advanced by Presidents Richard Nixon, Gerald Ford, and Jimmy Carter, this approach mainly involved extensive negotiations with our chief competitor, the Soviet Union, to limit strategic and conventional weapons. Reagan argued that we were not in a strong position to do so and looked desperate for an agreement, and therefore any outcome from détente would be detrimental to our interests. He disrupted conventional thinking, essentially arguing that détente was a national security approach of "peace through weakness."

Reagan proposed instead scrapping détente, building up U.S. military capability, shoring up our alliances, and then reapproaching the USSR, negotiating from a position of strength. The reaction to this was swift and critical. Opponents from both political parties cast him as dangerously naïve and a threat to world peace.

Yet in the face of that challenge and with the mainstream media and the pundit class further denigrating him, Reagan persisted— ever the "happy warrior" for freedom.

The late 1970s were difficult for our country. President Jimmy Carter had low favorability ratings due to widespread disaffection over low economic performance and a perception of U.S. weakness abroad (the Iran hostage crisis reinforced that view). This contributed to Reagan's decisive victory in 1980, and he immediately went to work to turn things around. Reagan's leadership personally inspired me. I enlisted shortly after he was inaugurated to be part of this cause of restoring American strength and respect around the world.

Over the next eight years President Reagan led our country and the world to a better place. In 1985, once U.S. military capability and readiness were restored, he returned to the negotiating table and won decisive concessions from the Soviets. We went beyond limiting, to *reducing* strategic and conventional arms, without giving up the Strategic Defense Initiative (SDI), a new program designed to protect us from incoming intercontinental ballistic missiles. With these bold diplomatic moves, Reagan seized the initiative. Throughout the late 1980s, the Soviets tried desperately to keep up with us, but the weight of their failing economy, exacerbated by the cost of financing combat operations in Afghanistan, required major readjustments in Warsaw Pact security policy, including the loosening of their control over Eastern and Central Europe. This emboldened democratic movements throughout the Warsaw Pact, including the Solidarity movement in Poland, which sensed real opportunity for seismic political change. Soviet "glasnost" reform policies designed to shore up political support for communist rule while staving off bankruptcy eventually backfired. With a taste of freedom, people throughout the Soviet bloc pressured for an end to communism.

I saw all of this up close and personal. My first duty assignment in the regular Army was with the Berlin Brigade from 1986 to 1989, and I was only fifty yards away from President Reagan when he gave his famous speech at the Berlin Wall challenging Soviet leader Gorbachev to "tear down this wall." It was a truly incredible moment. Upon hearing him utter those words, I remember thinking, "Wow, that was a powerful statement." Then my next thought was, "But that will never happen in my lifetime." How wrong I turned out to be, as only two and a half years later the Berlin Wall came down, marking the end of an era.

I learned two important lessons from that experience. First, "peace through strength" works. It's highly unlikely that détente would have produced those stunning positive results. Second, what a remarkable difference one person—with a powerful vision, strong communication skills, and the moral courage to lead—can make. An interesting postscript only reinforces this point. Years later, when I was assigned as a national security affairs fellow with the Hoover Institution at Stanford University, I met Reagan's speechwriter for the Berlin event. Peter Robinson, a Dartmouth graduate and Hoover fellow, shared with me that Reagan had written that powerful line into one of the early drafts of the speech. Concerned that it was too confrontational, senior White House staff removed it. That dynamic continued over several subsequent drafts. Every time the line was deleted, Reagan resolutely penciled it back in. He held his ground, and in the end it stayed. To this day, that direct challenge, and the results it yielded in ending the Cold War, is considered among his finest achievements. That's leadership.

With a disposable camera, I snapped this photo of President Reagan in Berlin, June 1987, challenging Soviet leader Gorbachev to "tear down this wall."

No More Vietnams

Since "neoconservatives" sometimes inaccurately claim President Reagan as among their adherents, one more vignette is needed to clarify the record—the American experience in Lebanon in 1983. I was a freshman at Siena College then and enrolled in the Army ROTC program while simultaneously a member of the New York Army National Guard. I remember vividly the contentious debate on campus about U.S. policy toward Lebanon. President Reagan had sent a sizable U.S. Marine Corps contingent to Beirut in an attempt to establish peace among the warring factions in that country's civil war. In October, things went very badly. Hezbollah, a new terrorist group at the time, pulled off a devastating suicide attack against our Marine barracks, killing 241 U.S. service members.

Americans were shocked, saddened, and in disbelief. Many on our campus and across the country expected Reagan to escalate in Lebanon. He did just the opposite. Cognizant of our recent history in Vietnam, and appreciating the complexity of the Middle East, he pulled our troops out. While this decision initially seemed to his critics to be out of character, they fundamentally misunderstood Reagan's approach to national security. He did not want to get us involved in a protracted land war in the Middle East that could cost many American lives and significantly drain the treasury when at the end of all that investment we might end up no better than when we started. Instead, he painfully cut his losses. Even in the midst of crisis, Reagan never lost perspective that winning the Cold War was the top priority for our national security and freedom. It was a wise decision to avoid another Vietnam, although he took a political hit at the time for withdrawing from Lebanon. Years later, when the Berlin Wall came down and the Soviet Union dissolved, it was clear—Reagan was right. Through his leadership and commitment to peace through strength, ultimately we became safer and more prosperous.

Defining Deterrence

The "peace through strength" approach places much weight on the complex subject of deterrence. For clarity, then, some definitions are in order. While large books have been written on it in the past, there is a simple explanation for deterrence and why nations act the way they do. I'll use North Korea to illustrate. Although there has been a truce in place since 1954 that suspended the Korean War, a long-term peace treaty has never been reached. North Korea's strongest preference would be a treaty that unites their country with South Korea under unified communist control. Given that desire, why does North Korea not attack South Korea? Because they are nice guys? Certainly, there is no evidence for that. North Korea does not attack South Korea (for the moment, anyway) because they believe the *costs outweigh the benefits* of such a course of action. That's deterrence.

For deterrence to work, national leaders must be able to acquire and process information and make determinations about costs and benefits for potential courses of action. They must also be able to perceive the status of their competitors' military and nonmilitary power and, in the Delphic sense, their own. Transparency is essential to keeping the peace. Nations unable to perceive the strength of a potential adversary could escalate out of fear, potentially provoking an unnecessary war.

When assessing strength, two broad factors matter—*capability* and *will*. Capability includes all elements of national power—military, diplomatic, economic, and informational. For deterrence, what matters is perceived capability. Of course, if deterrence fails and nations fight each other, only actual capability matters. Thus nations that bluff about their capabilities take on significant (potentially catastrophic) risk. At the same time, when improvements to capability are developed, it is in a nation's best interest to ensure that others know it. That is why it is common practice to invite potential adversaries to major training exercises. These actions strengthen deterrence.

Capability alone, however, does not achieve deterrence. A nation must possess the requisite *will* to employ that capability, if necessary. The fact is, if you have capability and do not have will, you don't have deterrence. Likewise, if you have will but don't have capability, you don't have deterrence. Expressions of national will come from both a nation's leaders and its people. For leaders, "video must equal audio." What you do has to match with what you say and vice versa. If a national leader draws a line in the sand and then doesn't enforce it, national will is weakened. Likewise, if a national leader expresses a position and potential adversaries don't perceive support for that position among the nation's people, that also undermines the perception of will (think the American experience in Vietnam after the Tet offensive).

The reality for the United States today is that our deterrence is lacking in both categories—capability and will. This atrophying of deterrence explains why we seem to have so many hot spots around the world. We are facing strategic challenges simultaneously from Russia, China, North Korea, and Iran.

Understanding deterrence in this way, one can see why switching to an isolationist approach in the face of these challenges is not the right decision for our country. Diplomatic disengagement gives the perception of diminished national will, weakening deterrence, potentially engendering more aggression on the part of our adversaries. Over the past decade, weakened U.S. deterrence has already hurt some of our friends and allies, like Ukraine, Georgia, Israel, and the Philippines, who have suffered aggression from Russia in the first two cases, and Hamas and China in the third and fourth. If trends of weakness and appeasement persist, deterrence could fail, leading to war. We've learned that much from history. The desperate effort to keep the peace at all costs was the reasoning behind the Munich Agreement in 1938, but that did not stop Hitler. In the end, failing to confront aggression led to war.

For successful deterrence, we need to restore capability and will and get the judgment right. We should reject both preemption and isolation. Both are bad choices when it comes to maximizing our liberty and security. This is exactly why as conservatives we must lead. We must restore founding principles that support peace through strength.

Sun Tzu—Still Relevant

For deterrence to work we must understand the relative strengths and weaknesses of potential adversaries, friends, and ourselves. Many centuries ago the Chinese military strategist and philosopher Sun Tzu exhorted, "Know your enemy." That still holds true today, and the current global landscape is daunting. The list of serious competitors and potential adversaries includes Russia, China, North Korea, and Iran. Beyond these nation-states, we face existential threats from radical Islamic terrorists and our own national debt.

Russia, arguably our most dangerous and aggressive potential foe, has made significant improvements in both its conventional and strategic forces in recent years. Russia's new main battle tank rivals our own, replete with advanced guns, optics, maneuverability, and protection. It is formidable in any fight. Additionally, Russia has improved the way it develops human talent. Unlike the Soviets I trained to face as a young Army officer in Europe in the late 1980s, the new Russian army emphasizes leader development and soldier initiative. Doctrine, too, has evolved—it is much more aggressive, taking advantage of improvements in human talent and technology. The Russian leader, Vladimir Putin, plays up nationalism, relying on external threats to keep control over his people. He has also shown a willingness to use newer capabilities, including the cyber domain, to wage hybrid warfare in places like Georgia, Ukraine, and Syria, and intimidation tactics in the Baltics. It is clear—U.S. deterrence is not working with Russia.

China surprised the Obama administration when in 2009 it started more aggressive naval activity in the South China Sea. The Chinese have followed that up with statements and actions (their so-called South China Sea "nine-dash line" policy) that encroach on the territorial seas and economic claims of regional neighbors, including the Philippines. Even after an unfavorable international court decision, China remains defiant and committed to moving forward with militarizing man-made "islands" in the Spratly chain. The Obama administration's response (the "pivot to the Asia-Pacific") has not worked. China continues to modernize its military and expand its offensive capabilities (including aircraft carriers) and has specialized in advanced antiship missiles that threaten our naval assets. All of these actions create "anti-access" challenges for us as we pursue our economic interests in that region and fulfill our treaty obligations with our allies. All that said, I do not believe we are destined to fight China, but for the purposes of assessing deterrence now, it's clear it is failing.

China's dysfunctional cousin, North Korea, remains a major problem for us, the region, and the world. Since the 1990s, our government has engaged in diplomatic activities intended to convince North Korea to give up its nuclear program in return for economic assistance and an invitation to join the community of nations. Despite these efforts, every so often we end up in crisis over further expansion of that North Korean nuclear weapons program. Not surprising, given our weakening capability and will, we are in one of those strategic moments now. North Korea has test-fired missiles that have landed close to Japanese shores and has had occasional skirmishes with the South Korean military. North Korean leader Kim Jong-un defies everyone, including the United States and China, and continues to mistreat his own people. They are on a perilous path toward potential armed conflict, and efforts to deter them have not been successful to date.

Finally, Iran continues to be a challenge. Its leaders have declared us the "Great Satan" of the world and have stated that they want to wipe Israel off the face of the earth. Given this regime's track record of exporting terrorism in Lebanon and Yemen, extensive support for Hezbollah, and its military activities in Syria, Iraq, and other quarters of the globe, Iran must be confronted. In 2015, the Obama administration concluded an agreement with Iran to limit its nuclear weapons program. In the Congress, I opposed that deal, because verification provisions were weak and the agreement did not prevent Iran from supporting terrorism with the over $150 billion they would get from it. This agreement will only get worse over time and we already know it did not change Iranian views of us. The day after they ratified the agreement, Iran's supreme leader told his nation that nothing has changed. To them, we remain Satan. Their disdain for us was on display several months later when they took our sailors hostage—humiliating us on the world stage. Meanwhile, Iran continues rogue ballistic missile testing and modernization of their military. Unfortunately, here too, deterrence is not working.

While potential adversaries take advantage of our weakened position, we are also facing some threats that cannot be deterred. Transnational actors such as terrorist organizations and organized crime syndicates gain no benefits from a stabilized international order, and some like Al Qaeda and the Islamic State seek to destroy civilization so it can be replaced with a worldwide caliphate under Sharia law.

Just as it is a false choice to think that isolationism will preserve our liberty against aggressive nation-states, it is also a false choice to think we can just ignore radical Islamic terrorism. As Trotsky once opined, "You may not be interested in war, but war is interested in you." These jihadist organizations have declared war on us and are acting accordingly. We have no choice but to fight them and win. Later, after I describe what must be done to deter Russia, China, North Korea, and Iran, I will explain how to defeat the radical Islamic terrorists.

———

We also face an existential threat in our national debt. Former chairman of the Joint Chiefs Admiral Mike Mullen when testifying before the Armed Services Committee described the national debt as the number one threat to our national security. The top priority of government is to protect its people and their rights, but if we go into a debt spiral causing national bankruptcy, then life as we know it will cease to exist. Clearly, then, these are coequal priorities. We must at once strengthen our national security to protect our liberties *and* get back to a balanced budget.

Toward that end, here are some important facts. President Obama's fiscal year 2017 defense budget request was *$100 billion less* than what he had projected for that year back in fiscal year 2012. This means at least two things. First, to those who desire to cut the defense budget to help get back to a balanced budget— we've already done that substantially. That $100 billion figure represents a 15 percent reduction from a planned $700 billion to roughly $600 billion for fiscal year 2017. Second, although I am a committed defense reformer and budget deficit hawk, I believe this reduction has been just too steep. We overshot the target and now need to right-size the defense budget by increasing it approximately $30 billion a year for the next five years. That is why for the past two years I helped House leadership build bipartisan support to reverse the Obama administration's cuts to defense. We succeeded in adding back in over $20 billion in each year. Going forward, the Trump administration wants to lift the sequester for defense spending, and I support that move. As we work to improve readiness, we need more certainty to properly plan and allocate resources. Changes in the world since 2012 warrant such action.

Given that defense investments will need to rise over the next five years, it is paramount that Congress scrutinize Pentagon management and force more reforms upon them to ensure we are getting maximum value for each dollar and to find savings wherever possible. Indeed, according to a 2016 report in the *Washington Post*, outside consultants claim to have found about $25 billion a year in fraud, waste, and abuse. If true, that would essentially pay for our new readiness requirements. Fortunately, Congress has already taken action in this area over the past several years, enacting significant reforms that will save the taxpayers a great deal of money in the long run. Among these is the requirement that the Department of Defense pass an external audit. This is long overdue. This country spends over $600 billion a year on national security in the base budget and overseas contingency account, and we must know where every penny goes. An external audit is the first step.

Our committee also ushered in significant bipartisan acquisition reform. Championed by our chairman, Representative Mac Thornberry; the ranking member, Representative Adam Smith; and Representative Mike Conaway of Texas, these reforms place more responsibility and authority with the respective services and incentivize performance, while enhancing transparency and accountability. After the disturbing program development failures of the F-22 and F-35, something had to change. Both programs were years behind schedule and hundreds of billions of dollars over budget. As I write, the F-35 continues to experience problems with software and the pilot ejection system. Recent reforms are improving matters, but there is still much more to do. We must learn from the mistakes of the past. We need these acquisition reforms to produce savings that can be reinvested to enhance readiness.

The Weinberger-Powell Doctrine

As we restore "peace through strength" we need a clear vision for when we will use force. The best articulation of that is the Weinberger-Powell Doctrine. First delivered by President Reagan's secretary of defense Caspar Weinberger at the National Press Club on November 28, 1984, this doctrine had six main points:

- The United States should not commit forces to combat unless the vital national interests of the United States or its allies are involved.
- U.S. troops should only be committed wholeheartedly and with the clear intention of winning. Otherwise, troops should not be committed.
- U.S. combat troops should be committed only with clearly defined political and military objectives and with the capacity to accomplish those objectives.
- The relationship between the objectives and the size and composition of the forces committed should be continually reassessed and adjusted if necessary.
- U.S. troops should not be committed to battle without a "reasonable assurance" of the support of U.S. public opinion and Congress.
- The commitment of U.S. troops should be considered only as a last resort.

The Weinberger-Powell Doctrine demonstrates an excellent understanding of deterrence. From it we develop, field, and demonstrate

superior military capability to signal to potential adversaries that any
aggression on their part will fail. In addition to military capability, the
doctrine acknowledges the importance of national will. The people
and the Congress must be on the same page as the commander in
chief with regard to diplomacy and war.

Importantly, once credible deterrence is established, we are
able to lead with our greatest strengths—our ideas—as outlined
in our founding documents. On our best days, other countries
want to be like us because our way of life provides for the most
freedom and prosperity the world has ever known. Through
diplomacy, commerce, trade, and humanitarian actions we are
able to advance our interests and help our friends. However, all of
that hinges on credible deterrence, and that means the ability to
back up diplomacy with decisive military action, if required.

A Twenty-First-Century Military

From the previous sections, it's clear that we face formidable
challenges from conventional and strategic forces, including
nuclear-capable ballistic missiles and cyber threats. To protect our
people, we must be able to deter these threats, and that means
modernizing our military. Our potential adversaries must be convinced that we have superior joint concepts and combat-ready
forces that can dominate them in any situation. We enjoyed that
standing in the world for about a decade after Operation Desert
Storm, but today we appear weaker. Strengthening our military
must be the top priority of the Trump administration.

In the 2017 National Defense Authorization Act (NDAA),
Congress took steps to shore up military readiness. Significant
reforms were enacted in what was probably the most substantial

national defense legislation since the Goldwater-Nichols Act of 1986. Some of the highlights included:

- Increasing the power and authority in the chairman of the Joint Chiefs of Staff. Among these changes, the chairman is now authorized to reassign forces across the combatant commands to address national readiness needs. This will enhance unity of effort and readiness.
- Eliminating the Quadrennial Defense Review (QDR), which had grown unwieldy and excessively bureaucratic, and directing a new National Military Strategy development process that better incorporates congressional input and synchronizes actions among and across combatant commands.
- Significantly reforming the defense acquisitions process to save precious dollars that may be reinvested to increase readiness.
- Elevating U.S. Cyber Command (CYBERCOM) to a unified command to place more national priority on cyber security and protecting our information systems.
- Streamlining and reducing headquarters across the DoD and reducing the number of general officers. This should improve effectiveness, enable more troops to be put on the front lines, and produce significant savings that can be reinvested to enhance readiness.
- Reversing the Obama administration's drawdown of the armed forces. Stopping the planned elimination of over sixty thousand troops and adding to existing troop levels.
- Increasing funding for operations and maintenance accounts to address training deficiencies and maintenance shortfalls. This will directly improve readiness.

More reforms and investments will be needed to restore deterrence and defeat radical Islamic terrorism.

We have some big decisions ahead regarding our nuclear arsenal, which is commonly called the Triad since it consists of three components: land-based missiles, strategic bombers, and submarines capable of launching nuclear weapons. All components are aging and we are already having some difficulty maintaining readiness. Our potential adversaries see that, and to a degree this is weakening deterrence, which for many decades has been based on the concept of mutual assured destruction (MAD). MAD is the notion that a nuclear exchange would be so devastating for all sides, mankind, and the earth that no one could win a nuclear war. Given that, no one starts a nuclear war—MAD keeps the peace.

The deterrence of MAD only works if we have a *viable nuclear arsenal*. As we consider how best to meet that requirement, we must consider cost. The price tag to develop and field a new generation of land-based missiles and submarines capable of launching nuclear weapons is staggering—hundreds of billions of dollars, possibly a trillion when all is said and done. With $20 trillion in national debt already, and the possibility of a debt crisis real, this cannot be overlooked. The House Armed Services Committee ordered a study to provide recommendations on how best to address this matter. My initial thoughts are to develop a new strategic bomber, which has dual use for conventional missions, and to retain and modernize our current inventory of land-based missiles and *Ohio*-class submarines. Given our serious fiscal situation, this may be best, but I'm willing to wait for the committee's report before making a final determination.

We face a second major challenge regarding strategic deterrence—stopping further proliferation. In addition to those nations already in the "nuclear club," North Korea and Iran have nuclear ambitions.

In fact, North Korea has a limited capability now, and they continue to work on expanding it, including the ability to deliver these weapons over long distances. Iran has pledged to suspend and dismantle their military nuclear program, but skeptics have doubts about their actions and intentions. We can expect other nations, and terrorist organizations, to seek to acquire nuclear weapons, as well as radiological, chemical, and biological weapons. Since deterrence doesn't work on terrorist organizations, preventing them from getting these weapons is vital to our security. Finally, from this analysis, it is clear why fielding a *robust missile defense capability* is also a national priority.

President Reagan argued that relying exclusively on MAD as a form of deterrence is immoral for a Judeo-Christian nation. That is why he ordered the initiation of a national missile defense program. He stuck to its development in the face of significant pressure from the Soviets and widespread ridicule from the mainstream media and American left, who argued that he was pursuing science fiction. Yet today we have an operational West Coast missile defense capability in both Alaska and California. These missile sites are tied together with a joint advanced early warning system throughout the Pacific theater and national, global assets. We must broaden this capability. I support the East Coast missile defense program, which has been in development for a number of years, and should be ready for fielding soon. By adding this capability, we will have more robust, comprehensive coverage for our entire country. Given the intercontinental missile capability of our potential adversaries and the political instability in North Korea in particular, this is a must.

Since World War II, our military has enjoyed *air and sea dominance* during combat operations. This is no longer a given. Russia and China have fielded fifth-generation stealth fighters with the ability to contest the skies. Air dominance is critical to the success of land forces, and thus we will need to make further technological investments and adapt training strategies to stay ahead of our potential adversaries. Despite serious problems with development, the F-22 Raptor and the F-35 Joint Strike Fighter, which is a dual-purpose stealth fighter and ground strike platform presently in fielding, give us excellent fifth-generation capabilities to dominate the air. It's vitally important that we work out remaining problems with the F-35 and keep operations and maintenance accounts for both platforms properly funded to ensure they are combat ready.

With regard to our naval forces, we lack strategic reach. We are not able to maintain 365-day aircraft carrier coverage in our focus areas, experiencing periodic underlaps in the Mediterranean and Asia-Pacific regions. Our potential adversaries know that, and this is weakening deterrence. Accordingly, I support *increasing the number of naval aircraft carriers from eleven to twelve*. An aircraft carrier strike group is accompanied by cruisers, destroyers, and frigates, so we will need to procure more of them to fully fleet this new strike group.

Another major concern for sea dominance is the declining state of readiness of deployed carrier strike groups. We have too many aircraft down for maintenance deficiencies and pilots taking to the skies without proper training. The 2017 NDAA added funds to improve this situation, but more must be done. This decline in readiness has been correlated with an increase in major training accidents, some causing the death of pilots. It must be reversed.

The bottom line here is that our naval forces play a key strategic role, projecting power and overcoming anti-access challenges for our nation. In addition to putting airpower in position to achieve desired effects, they also deliver the U.S. Marine Corps, an essential component to land power dominance. Naval forces also move the preponderance of logistics that sustain land campaigns. When we enhance naval readiness and our potential adversaries perceive that, we strengthen deterrence.

This brings me to *strengthening land power.* In the 2017 NDAA, Congress significantly improved the readiness of our land forces. Most important, we stopped the Obama administration's planned drawdown. The administration was on track to reduce over 60,000 troops from Army and Marine Corps end strength by 2018. The regular Army, for example, would have shrunk to 450,000 troops, its lowest level since before World War II. This would have been a huge mistake that I helped stop.

In early 2016, working with Representative Tim Walz, Democrat of Minnesota, the highest-ranking enlisted man ever to serve in the U.S. House of Representatives, and Mike Turner of Ohio, we authored and introduced the Protecting Our Security Through Utilizing Right-Sized End-Strength Act, or for short, the Posture Act. It was necessary for several reasons. First, those planned reductions would have left us with force levels insufficient to meet war plan requirements, and our potential adversaries knew it. The real risk is that if we are required to fight a major-theater war against one of our potential adversaries, we would not have enough ready forces to defeat a second threat. At best, we might be able to "hold" in a second theater as we defeated the first potential adversary. That posture signaled weakness to Russia, China, North Korea, and Iran, and they are taking advantage of it already. Moreover, given the demands of fighting the Islamic State and other terrorist organizations, it's far from certain that we would be able to even meet the "defeat and hold" requirements at acceptable risk levels. Making matters worse, once a brigade is stood down, it can take over three years to reconstitute it given how long it takes to recruit, assess, train, and validate individual troops and brigades. It's not like a light switch you can turn off and on. Finally, with fewer troops, deployments for the ones remaining come at a faster pace, exacerbating mental health challenges for veterans and families. All of this equates to weaker deterrence.

In testimony before our committee, the Joint Chiefs expressed preliminary support for the Posture Act, but only if it came with the necessary funding to ensure that any new troops were properly trained and equipped. We listened and made that happen. Although Democratic minority leader Nancy Pelosi initially opposed my bill, we were able to gain enough House Democratic cosponsors to outflank her, including key support from combat veterans in their caucus, Representatives Tulsi Gabbard and Seth Moulton, along with my coauthor Walz. The NDAA conference report that the president signed in December 2016 included the Posture Act along with about $3 billion to ensure that readiness requirements for these new troops were addressed. Getting this done was a huge win for our military and a major step forward for strengthening land power and restoring peace through strength.

With the enactment of the Posture Act, we are presently at pre–September 11 troop levels (regular Army strength is 476,000 and active-duty Marine Corps is 183,000) and capable of executing our war plans at moderate risk. Going forward, I support modestly increasing end strength to further reduce risk to lower levels. We will need to add 14,000 troops to the regular Army to get to 490,000, and another 12,000 National Guard troops and 6,000 Army Reservists to achieve end strengths of 355,000 and 205,000, respectively, in those forces. The Marine Corps needs an additional 2,000 to get to 185,000. These added troops will lower risk and allow for more time at home station in between deployments. Just as with the Posture Act, any additional troops will need to come with additional funding to ensure optimal levels of unit manning, equipping, and training.

Some in Washington question the value of making these investments, but every time in our history when we significantly reduced or underfunded our land forces, we later regretted it. My generation of soldiers was keenly aware of that history. We had a saying that served as our rallying cry—"no more Task Force Smiths." This came from our failure during the first major engagement of the Korean War, the battle of Osan. During that fight one of our infantry battalions (1st Battalion, 21st Infantry Regiment), commanded by Lieutenant Colonel Charles B. Smith, was isolated, undermanned, and poorly trained, equipped, and led. They were completely decimated and overrun by North Korean tank regiments. It was an utter disaster, with very high casualties and complete mission failure. After World War II, the ranks of the Army were deeply reduced and the remaining forces were woefully underfunded, leaving them unprepared for combat in Korea. Ultimately our armed forces rallied from that rough start and performed well in battle after we properly manned, equipped, and trained them.

When peacetime preparation is done right, it makes all the difference. The U.S. military spent most of the late 1970s and entire 1980s perfecting "AirLand Battle" doctrine. This was a new approach to warfare that emphasized speed and synchronization to overwhelm potential adversaries. The new doctrine transformed our military, calling for changes in recruitment, organizational design and training, leader development, and equipment development and procurement. All of these initiatives were properly funded, and when next the call came to go to war, it was clear that the reforms paid off.

Defying the trend of bad performance in the opening battle
of a war, the U.S. military that fought in Panama in 1989 and
the Persian Gulf in 1991 completely destroyed their foe from
the outset. The decisive victory during Operation Desert Storm
was particularly noteworthy considering it was against an enemy
(Iraq) that possessed the fourth-largest military in the world at
the time. After an intensive and effective six-week bombing campaign, the ground war lasted only one hundred hours—a truly
remarkable feat.

I participated in that operation as a twenty-six-year-old captain in the 82nd Airborne Division and witnessed that when
properly resourced, AirLand Battle doctrine—the effective synchronization of air, land, and sea forces—produces dramatic victory. We truly achieved dominance, and that translated to both
operational and strategic success. Coalition forces routed the Iraqi
army and Kuwait was liberated. In the process, we suffered mini-
mal casualties. Every loss of life hurts, but keeping those numbers
under 150 killed in action was miraculous considering we were
up against an enemy who put hundreds of thousands of soldiers
in the field, many of whom had recent combat experience against
Iran, and considering that the number of Iraqis killed in action
has been estimated at more than 30,000. None of that would
have been possible if we hadn't strengthened land power in the
1980s.

Putting It All Together

All of these investments to strengthen military capability across
the respective services ultimately must come together in *joint
operational concepts and readiness* that support war plans. When

potential adversaries observe a training exercise in which we demonstrate the ability to strategically maneuver and fully support a campaign plan, it alters their thinking, deterring them from aggression. When they perceive that we have the ability to overcome anti-access, dominate the air and seas, and deliver joint forces with decisive overmatch, they will accept a diplomatic solution on our terms. In this way, we strengthen the hands of diplomats as they advance our interests abroad.

That joint employment concept begins with the Global Response Force (GRF). This is the nation's "911 capability," prepared to deploy anywhere in the world on twenty-four to forty-eight hours of notification. It includes elements from all of the services and is capable of forcible entry operations (parachute assault and amphibious landing). The GRF can secure initial objectives to pave the way for follow-on campaign forces in support of a major-theater war plan. The GRF can also deploy immediately to respond to natural disasters both here and abroad. I spent the preponderance of my military service with the GRF, including three command tours in the 82nd Airborne Division (at the company, battalion, and brigade levels). While serving on the GRF, I deployed my brigade to Haiti to assist with humanitarian relief operations in the immediate aftermath of the devastating earthquake there in 2010.

We must enhance readiness throughout the armed forces, because our war plans count on that. In the joint operational concept, after the GRF, early-arriving forces, including light infantry, Stryker, and heavy forces (Army and Marines), deploy to expand the lodgment in enemy territory. They are reinforced with campaign forces (including activated National Guard and Reserve forces) to achieve decisive victory in land combat. After more than fifteen years of persistent combat in difficult counterinsurgency conditions, we must now focus on restoring full-spectrum capabilities throughout the joint force.

All of these operations require state-of-the-art command and control capabilities and world-class logistical support. Especially important, to fully restore the joint operational concept, we will need to invest heavily in training, including increasing rotations at the national combat training centers. In peacetime it's hard to fully rehearse and train all of these joint capabilities and requirements, but this is where computer modeling and simulations and rigorous command post exercises can make a tremendous difference to validating war plans and enhancing readiness.

Joint operational readiness enhances diplomacy. A classic example of this occurred in 1994, when President Bill Clinton compelled the leader of a rogue military junta in Haiti, General Raoul Cédras, to relinquish power to the duly elected leader of that country. In late 1991, Cédras had ousted Jean-Bertrand Aristide, the democratically elected leader of Haiti. For years, he refused to give up power, defying his people and the community of nations. By September 1994, Clinton had organized significant international pressure to force Cédras to step down. As part of that, Clinton sent former president Jimmy Carter, U.S. senator Sam Nunn, and former chairman of the Joint Chiefs of Staff General Colin Powell to Haiti to convince him to leave. Cédras initially rebuffed this high-level delegation, until General Powell informed the rogue Haitian general that the 82nd Airborne Division was in the air preparing for a parachute assault on Port-au-Prince and that a joint force from the sea, including U.S. Marines and elements of the Army's 10th Mountain Division, was also en route to invade the country in order to forcefully remove him from power. Cédras was able to verify Powell's claim through images shown on CNN, and that was enough for him to yield. He immediately left Haiti, and Aristide was restored to power. This successful diplomacy was made possible by trained and ready joint forces.

Recent developments in NATO are an excellent example how enhanced joint operational readiness can bolster deterrence supporting a "peace through strength" approach. Responding to a 2015 Rand study that concluded NATO was not able to reinforce the Baltic nations (Estonia, Latvia, and Lithuania) fast enough to stop a Russian invasion, the fiscal year 2017 NDAA provided additional troops and funding to address that shortfall. Our troops are part of a new plan called Enhanced Forward Presence (EFP) that stations NATO forces in the Baltics and a U.S. armored brigade in Poland.

By shoring up NATO now, we hope to deter further Russian aggression, keeping the peace in Europe. Twice in the twentieth century, the United States pursued policies of isolationism, trying to stay neutral in world wars. It didn't work. Eventually we were drawn in to those conflicts, at great cost to American life and treasure. *By standing with NATO now and deterring Russia, we hope to prevent World War III.* That is peace through strength.

———

During the summer of 2016, while I and my fellow representatives were fighting to ensure that the Posture Act was included in the final version of the NDAA, I led an overseas bipartisan congressional delegation (CODEL) trip to highlight the importance of our bill and to hear directly from NATO and U.S. European Command leaders. The trip included stops in four countries—Israel, Poland, Latvia, and Germany. The delegation included my Democratic cochair, Representative Dan Lipinski of Illinois (also the leader of the Polish-American Caucus); from the House Armed Services Committee, Republican representatives Austin Scott of Georgia, Paul Cook of California, and Rich Nugent of Florida; from the Joint Select Intelligence Committee, Chris Stewart of Utah; and from the Veterans Affairs Committee, Dan Benishek of Michigan. The Army provided the escort support, with Major Pat McGuigan as the officer in charge. Our spouses accompanied us at no cost to the U.S. government (members were responsible for their expenses).

The first stop was in Israel to receive briefings on the Trophy Active Protection System fielded by the Israel Defense Forces (IDF) along the Lebanese and Syrian borders. Trophy is a reactive armor system placed on vehicles and tanks to protect them. As part of the Posture Act, our delegation supported outfitting the U.S. armored brigade deploying to Poland with Trophy. It was a three-hour van ride from Jerusalem to the Golan region, where we transferred into armored vehicles to visit an IDF company outpost along the Lebanese border. From this concrete-reinforced bunker, we had a panoramic view of previous tank battles and skirmishes between IDF and Hezbollah forces over the years as we received an impressive briefing on the Trophy system. Only recently fielded, this system has already saved lives. In addition to protecting Israeli vehicles with the reactive armor, the system has RF antennas enabling Trophy to determine exact enemy locations, allowing IDF soldiers to immediately return fire to kill the attackers. Trophy has had a transformative effect on the battlefield and the psyche of enemy fighters. The IDF now has the initiative. Our delegation discussed all this (and more) when we met with Israeli prime minister Benjamin Netanyahu the following day.

With Prime Minister Netanyahu. Also pictured are my wife, Mary Jo, Representative Chris Stewart, and his wife, Evie. *Credit: Prime Minister Netanyahu's Office*

We next went to Poland. Getting NATO nations to pay more for their own defense is a major U.S. priority, and Poland is leading the way on this issue. The country already spends more than the NATO-required 2 percent of GDP on defense, and expects to reach 3 percent soon. Given their history and proximity to Russia, the Poles are obviously concerned about Putin's actions and intentions. We had frank discussions with the Polish deputy foreign minister, Marek Ziółkowski, and deputy defense minister, Tomasz Szatkowski, on this issue, and they expressed their gratitude for U.S. leadership and NATO's EFP plan.

From there we flew to Latvia, one of the three Baltic nations very anxious about Russia's involvement in that region. Foreign Minister Edgars Rinkēvičs and Defense State Secretary Jānis Garisons highlighted those concerns during our meetings, bringing home the fact that during World War II the country was occupied by the Soviet Union and the memory of that traumatic experience pervades Latvian consciousness to this day. With recent Russian aggression in Georgia and Ukraine, Latvia has taken steps to significantly increase the size and readiness of its armed forces. The Latvians deeply appreciate our partnership and look forward to welcoming a Canadian battalion in 2017 as part of EFP. In the meantime, a U.S. armored battalion commanded by Army lieutenant colonel Johnny Evans was on deployment, training with Latvian armed forces. We met with Lieutenant Colonel Evans and received his assessment. Evans also emphasized the importance of the "Suwalki Gap" connecting Poland with Lithuania. If the Russians ever get control of it, NATO would not be able to maneuver forces to reinforce Baltic nations under attack.

From Latvia, we flew to our final destination, Wiesbaden, Germany, where we met with NATO supreme allied commander, Europe (SACEUR), General Curtis "Mike" Scaparrotti, and Lieutenant General Ben Hodges and attended the annual Senior Commanders' Conference. At the conference, General Scaparrotti provided his vision and made it clear: Europe was in transition, ramping up to meet the Russian challenge. Nested with national political objectives of increasing defense expenditures from other NATO nations, the SACEUR exhorted his subordinates to help allied forces enhance their capacity and readiness.

Both General Scaparrotti and Lieutenant General Hodges explained how NATO would strengthen deterrence over the next year. The major piece was the deployment of a U.S. armored brigade to Poland and the shipment of two additional sets of brigade equipment that would be prepositioned (without troops) in Europe, to further reinforce NATO capabilities. General Scaparrotti believed that those actions, along with the additional troop deployments in the Baltics by other NATO nations, would reestablish deterrence—causing Putin to take pause.

Attending the Commanders' Conference and hearing directly from NATO leaders helped our members to better appreciate how reinforcing Europe secured U.S. interests. These actions should stabilize the political situation and preclude another war. The feedback we received from frontline commanders also strengthened our arguments for the Posture Act and played an important role in helping us prevail on this issue in conference with the Senate later that fall.

One final point: For Republicans, we must be able to take yes for an answer. Many of us, including myself, have been saying for years that we need our NATO allies to step up and do more for their own defense. Now, in large part because of our leadership, they are doing just that. More NATO nations than ever are meeting their 2 percent defense investment requirement, and more still (twenty-one of twenty-eight) have publicly pledged to increase defense investments. Now is not the time to back away from Europe. If we do so and Russia continues their aggression, we increase the chances of World War III.

"Lines in the Sand"

Deterrence equals capability and will. To strengthen deterrence and the "peace through strength" approach, we must take steps to address shortcomings in the perception of our political will.

Political will begins with national leadership. The commander in chief must provide the vision to reform and strengthen the military, set the framework for functional and effective civil-military relations, work well with the Congress to ensure proper funding levels and policies, and communicate clearly in developing situations.

Quite frankly, just as we have experienced a declining military capacity from overuse in the past fifteen-plus years, we have also seen eroding political will, in part because of ineffective executive leadership and dysfunctional civil-military relations. The most obvious (and painful) example of lack of will on the part of national leaders occurred when President Barack Obama drew a "line in the sand" regarding Syrian use of chemical weapons, and then when the Assad regime crossed it, we did nothing. That clearly displayed a lack of resolve, and it hurt our deterrence everywhere, not just in Syria.

The budget standoff between the Obama administration and Congress, which has resulted in sequestration (rigid across-the-board spending reductions, including DoD accounts, to comply with the top-line spending limits of the 2011 Budget Control Act), has also weakened our national will in the perception of our friends, allies, and potential adversaries.

We are now at a point where we have stumbled for many years with improper command guidance, dysfunctional civil-military relations, inadequate funding, and poor crisis decision making. The lack of military experience among our national leaders is showing. We need a new direction, leaders who know what they are doing. In the near future, we need to elect a president with combat experience. Due to their experiences, veterans understand teamwork, sacrifice, being part of something greater than themselves, and mission accomplishment. These are traits and experiences that may also help the nation come together and heal, as well as find a voice of reason in our politics. With the passing of time, we should see a new crop of combat veterans prepared for presidential candidacy, and I look forward to that occurring. Just over the horizon I can see several leaders in the Republican ranks who fit that description now—Ryan Zinke, Steve Russell, Tom

Cotton, Martha McSally, Lee Zeldin, and Eric Greitens, just to name a few. Many more are coming. The Democrats have Seth Moulton and Tulsi Gabbard gaining in national stature, making the competition interesting. National leaders with combat experience should help our "peace through strength" approach.

The final factor contributing to national political will pertains to us—*we the people*. As citizens, we have rights *and* responsibilities. Citizens play an important role in the expression of national will. The degree to which we support our national leaders in challenging times and the extent to which we volunteer to personally contribute to the effort plays a role in how our friends, allies, and potential adversaries perceive our strength. In World War II, the perception of our national unity and resolve was strong for all to see, and that made a positive difference. During the Vietnam War, the opposite was true, almost from the start, certainly by late 1966 or early 1967, and that also made a difference—but not in a good way.

That is certainly not to suggest that as citizens we should follow our leaders blindly. We are a self-governing people and should be critical consumers of information, expressing ourselves regularly. My point is that there is an important interactive dynamic between the leaders and the led, and our policies should reflect that reality. There is an essential role for leaders to play in shaping public opinion and inspiring us to do hard things that are in our best interests, but there is a fine line between that and national leaders who, after much dialogue between the leaders and the led, insist on taking us where the people don't want to go. In the latter case, we just need new leaders. Harmonizing that dynamic and getting it right is essential to expressing strong national will. On that score, the Weinberger-Powell Doctrine is the best expression. U.S. troops should only be committed to war when the support of the Congress and the American people can be assured.

National leaders have a critical responsibility to communicate and build consensus for any proposed military action, if vital interests are at stake, and only if all other means to achieve those interests have been tried and exhausted. Similarly, the American people have a responsibility to be conversant and informed about the issues and to express their views on potential courses of action. We decide as a nation, which is precisely why our Founders intended for the people's representatives in Congress to make the call when we go to war. Once committed, the American people should stand by those choices until victory is achieved. Leaders must always be assessing the status of campaigns and the degree of public support to determine if changes of plan are possible or required to achieve the desired end state while preserving the national political will. If wide gaps emerge between leaders and the led, expect our adversaries to exploit them. They have done so effectively in the past.

In a representative democracy, these realities are unavoidable. This is all the more reason why judgment matters. Experience matters too. We need leaders with both. The absence of these two traits in our national leaders has caused us significant problems. We have been too quick to use military force since the end of World War II, and many of the big problems we face today can be attributed that. Going forward we must reject the failed policies of preemption and embrace once again the "peace through strength" approach that relies on deterrence.

Defeating Radical Islamic Terrorists

Unfortunately, some threats cannot be deterred. Radical Islamic terrorism is one of them. Since they have declared war on us and are acting as such, they can't be ignored—they must be defeated. As we ponder the most effective way to accomplish that, it is important to first examine this enemy's strengths and weaknesses. In terms of their strengths, this radical jihadist movement has gained momentum by claiming they are addressing long-standing unrest in the Muslim world. They claim leadership in the Muslim world for those desiring to live by the Koran and to have a more flourishing existence. That approach, as fraudulent as it is, has worked. For many years the radical Islamic terrorists have been flush with financial supporters and volunteer fighters, including those ready to martyr themselves for the cause. Undermining that present strength is key to our success.

Let's take a closer look at the rise of the Islamic State. To me there can be no doubt that there is a lot of blame to go around as to how we let this terrorist group get so formidable. The immediate cause was the Obama administration's incompetence and lack of political will to use its considerable leverage to ensure that Iraqi prime minister Nouri al-Maliki continued on the path we help set during and immediately after the Surge of 2007. By 2009, Iraq looked poised to stabilize and offer a better life for its people. Insurgent attacks were largely nonexistent, the military professionalism of the Iraqi Security Forces (ISF) was on the rise, and the economy was showing signs of growth and possibility. With the oil fields throughout the country beginning to return to prewar capacity, the treasury was flush with resources too. Things were looking up.

A lot of focus has been placed on whether U.S. troops should have stayed in Iraq longer. In my view, that was not the key error of the Obama administration. It is worth pointing out even after we withdrew our combat units, the number of troops supporting the U.S. embassy in Baghdad was the largest of any diplomatic mission in the world. The biggest mistake we made during the first term of the Obama administration was not using our leverage to insist that any future U.S. support (military, financial, economic, and diplomatic) was entirely contingent on Iraqi leadership properly supporting the trained ISF in the field and continuing on the path of national reconciliation with the Sunnis and Kurds. Absent that behavior, we should have withdrawn all support. I'm convinced that had we exerted that influence, Prime Minister Maliki would have sustained the readiness levels of all of his security forces—not just the perceived loyal Shia-dominated units. Politically, this would have changed the direction of Iraqi politics too. Instead of pursuing criminal charges against the highest-ranking Iraqi Sunni, Vice President Tariq al-Hashimi, and stonewalling the Kurds on the question of oil revenue-sharing policies, Maliki would have seen it in his interests to continue on the path of national reconciliation that we helped them establish after the Surge. When the U.S. government did not insist on reconciliation, Maliki viewed that as tacit approval for his sectarian approach, and these harsh policies continued for years.

Islamic State forces grew in strength and capability, fighting Assad during the Syrian Civil War. In 2014, these forces crossed the Iraqi border and marched on Mosul, the second-largest city in Iraq. The Iraqi Security Forces there (largely comprised of Sunni and Kurdish soldiers), after seeing their competent commanders fired for political reasons and having no money for weapons, ammunition, training, and logistical support, simply removed their uniforms and left their posts. They were not willing to die for a government that did not represent them—worse, that abused them. The Islamic State took advantage of the situation and provided an alternative for disaffected Sunnis to the corrupt and wicked Iraqi government. That was the proximate cause for the rise of the Islamic State in Iraq in 2014.

That is not the whole story, however. Contributing to the rise of the Islamic State were the U.S. government's earlier decisions to pursue regime change in Iraq and Libya. These actions helped the Islamic State and other international jihadist organizations gain support throughout the Muslim world and provided a safe haven from which to launch further attacks.

The decision to invade Iraq in 2003 was a mistake. It certainly cannot be justified from a "peace through strength" approach. Iraq was not responsible for the September 11 attacks. Iraq did not attack our country. While an approach of peace through strength may include taking military action if our enemy is in the process of attacking us, that was not the case here. In fact, the Bush administration never claimed an attack was imminent. What they argued was that Iraq had weapons of mass destruction, was evil, and *could* attack us. Such were the circumstances with the USSR throughout the Cold War, but that was not cause to attack them.

We must see the 2003 invasion for what it was—a change in the strategic direction of our country. President Bush signaled that this was coming in his speech to graduating cadets at the U.S. Military Academy at West Point in May 2002. There, he made the case for "preemption"—the idea that we were prepared to end regimes viewed as potential threats. Regime change in Iraq led to occupation, playing right into the narrative of radical Islamic terrorists, who painted us among Muslims as invaders bent on secularizing their nation. This produced more funding and recruits for jihad, making our task of defeating the extremists harder. Deviating from peace through strength has left us less secure, worsened our debt crisis, and created a crisis in veterans' care that we will endure for decades. It also contributed to the rise of the Islamic State.

Barack Obama won the presidency in 2008 in large measure

due to his opposition of the Iraq invasion. Yet only three years later he led the country on a regime-change folly of his own. The military intervention in March 2011, which the United States supported, deposed Libyan president Muammar Gaddafi. In the immediate aftermath, international efforts to establish a viable new government failed, and the country soon became an ungoverned space that jihadist organizations exploited. From safe havens within Libya, terrorist training and support activities soon followed. These developments enabled the deadly attack on our Benghazi consulate on September 11, 2012, during which U.S. ambassador Chris Stevens, diplomatic officer Sean Smith, and two former Navy SEALs, Tyrone Woods and Glen Doherty, were killed. My party is very upset over the entire Benghazi ordeal. So am I—but the best way to avoid future Benghazis is to not go to Libya in the first place. Subsequently, from their safe havens in Libya, the Islamic State was able to train recruits and then send them to Syria and Iraq, which significantly helped their 2014 offensive.

The Islamic State's greatest strength is also its biggest vulnerability, because its entire movement to "help" Muslims is based on fraud. It claims it is advancing the cause of Muslims, but the reality is that no one kills more Muslims than the Islamic State. In areas where it has established control, Sharia law has worsened the plight of the people. Ultimately Muslims living under the Islamic State have less liberty, less security, and more brutality and misery. Recognizing that reality and exploiting it is key to our success. I'll share a story from my time in Iraq to illustrate how we exploited this vulnerability against Al Qaeda in Iraq (AQI), the predecessor of the Islamic State.

I served as the 25th Infantry Division operations officer during the Surge in 2007. That summer we conducted offensive operations to take back from AQI hamlets in the Diyala River valley and Baqubah, the seat of government of the province. One of our ground units in Baqubah was a Stryker brigade commanded by Colonel (now Lieutenant General) Steve Townsend. They worked well with the local populace and as a result benefited from intelligence received from Sunni Muslims disaffected with AQI.

One incredibly hot day in July (the temperature was over 125 degrees) I received a call from my longtime friend Lieutenant Colonel Fred Johnson, Colonel Townsend's deputy commander, informing me that a man claiming to be the leader of the local insurgent group had just entered his headquarters looking for help to defeat AQI. I wasn't sure what to make of this at first, because Fred and I had a history of practical jokes, and this one sounded too good to be true. Fred assured me this was legit— "This guy is ready to take it to AQI." Fred then conveyed that the insurgent leader had said, "We don't know what we want. We're not crazy about you and we'll deal with that later, but we know what we *don't* want. We don't want Al Qaeda." The insurgent gave accounts of their suffering under AQI rule. They were cutting off the fingers of people caught smoking, taking teenage girls as part of their harem, and holding Sharia court in the village square, in some cases summarily executing local villagers. This caused the Sunni tribal leaders to turn against AQI. They were ready to fight them and wanted help.

This insurgent leader provided locations for known AQI fighters. Colonel Townsend approved a plan to support these local Iraqis in their attack, providing them with Army physical training (PT) reflective belts so that our attack helicopter pilots could distinguish them in the fight that ensued. Supported by our airpower, they destroyed those AQI fighters.

Quite frankly, this was a weird experience at first, getting in

league with the same folks who only recently had been trying
to kill us. But a new reality was emerging. Similar to what had
happened the previous year in Anbar Province, Sunni sheiks in
Diyala Province and throughout Iraq were switching sides. Disaffected with AQI, they were ready to give the new Iraq a chance.
This movement has been labeled the "Sunni Awakening," and it
played a pivotal role in the success of the Surge.

Working with Sunni leaders in Iraq in 2006–7, we exploited
the fraudulent nature of AQI, which left them isolated and vulnerable. Local Iraqis increasingly provided intelligence and local support that led to their demise. AQI later morphed into the Islamic
State, but they are vulnerable for the same reasons. If their fraudulent nature can be exposed, they can be isolated and defeated.

With Lieutenant Colonel Fred Johnson, deputy commander, 3-2 Stryker, in Baqubah,
Iraq, rebuilding police headquarters.

Going forward, we always reserve the right to act immediately and unilaterally to defeat an imminent terrorist attack on our country. In the absence of an imminent attack, the smartest approach is to support Muslim nations and peoples taking the fight to the Islamic State, because this exposes their fraudulent nature, making it harder for these jihadists to secure financial backing and attract recruits.

Helping Iraq and the Iraqi Kurds retake Mosul was a good first step. The Iraqi government should now exploit that success and complete the destruction of the Islamic State in their country. The United States should continue to assist by providing weapons, ammunition, logistical support, airpower, intelligence support, and teams of advisers. We should also urge Iraqi prime minister Haider al-Abadi's government to translate recent operational gains into good governance and work diligently toward national reconciliation. Let's use our leverage and learn from the mistakes of the past.

In Syria, we should be fully engaged diplomatically to help forge an interim peace agreement. These negotiations will be delicate, given the differing agendas among the Assad regime, rebels (those not associated with AQI, the Islamic State, or affiliates), Kurds, Turkey, Russia, and other partners in the region. Our focus should be on getting an interim peace agreement, not insisting on regime change—ultimately that will be a decision for the Syrian people. Once an interim agreement is reached, we will have the necessary political foundation to support combat operations in a manner similar to how we supported Iraq and the Iraqi Kurds, to complete the destruction of the Islamic State.

As we accomplish all of these critical tasks, we should keep in mind a couple of important points. First, it is counterproductive for the United States to occupy territory in a Muslim country. By doing so we only reinforce the false narrative that radical jihadists spread about the United States—that we are there to occupy them and transform their country into a secular nation. Such actions facilitate jihadist recruitment and fund-raising efforts. With well over a billion people who adhere to the Muslim faith, we must avoid the misperception that we are at war with all Muslims. We should be working through our Sunni Muslim friends to defeat this fraudulent and evil enemy.

Second, protecting our people from terrorist attacks also requires securing our borders and competently administering our refugee and visa programs. In Congress, I voted for bills that supported all of these priorities. The vetting process for refugees and visa applicants requires improvement. As we proceed on this course, reforms should be based on security standards, not religion. Under the Constitution, we can deny entry to anyone attempting to come here if we believe they are a security risk, but to deny entry to a class of people strictly based on a particular faith does not reflect the values of a country founded upon religious liberty.

By taking all of the steps outlined in this section, we will defeat the terrorists and keep our people safe in a manner consistent with the Constitution and our values.

Looking Forward

Being a witness to President Reagan's iconic speech at the Brandenburg Gate in Berlin and hearing him call on Soviet leader Gorbachev to "tear down this wall" was a watershed moment for me. Reagan's passionate defense of liberty and actions to advance freedom around the world shaped my worldview. The genius of Reagan was that he could look over the horizon and see possibilities others could not. He also had keen self-awareness and a mix of humility and self-confidence. That type of leadership is rare and special, and we desperately need it now.

The battle for freedom at the Berlin Wall is over. We won. Now we face new challenges. We see the possibility of a resurgent Russia driven by nationalistic forces and an aggressive authoritarian leader, an ambitious China in pursuit of resources beyond its borders, diabolical forces in Iran and North Korea with apocalyptic designs for humanity, and a warped and violent version of Islam exploiting alienated Muslim youths around the world.

We are at a crossroads. Fortunately, we have a time-tested approach, one that decisively won Desert Storm and prevailed during the Cold War, to help us in these challenging times. By strengthening military capability and national will, we will enhance deterrence. Our potential adversaries will respond to those moves and check their aggressive behavior. By empowering Sunni Muslim nations and peoples to defeat Islamic extremism, we will neutralize jihadist capabilities while denying them access to the funding and recruits they need to carry forward their cause. Finally, by restoring peace through strength we will be able to keep our people safe while staying true to our values. The authoritarians of the left and the right cannot compete with us in the space of ideas—Reagan's message at the Berlin Wall is still as relevant today as it was then.

CHAPTER 2

Restore Founding Principles

The Spirit of Philadelphia

As he was departing Independence Hall in Philadelphia following the conclusion of the Constitutional Convention in September 1787, Ben Franklin was asked by a lady, "What have we got?" Franklin replied, "A republic, if you can keep it." While Franklin had a well-earned reputation for sharp wit, this was a serious comment. A careful reader of history, he was fully aware of the seemingly inescapable vicious cycle that had beset previous great republics over the ages, including Greece and Rome. The pattern was all too familiar. These republics moved through phases from founding and rise, to sustained stability and prosperity, followed by eventual fiscal and moral decay, then fall. Thus even if we were able to overcome the significant political challenges of the founding era to establish ourselves as a viable and flourishing republic, over time the odds would be against us.

Indeed, today many Americans wonder if our republic will long endure. Public confidence in institutions is at all-time lows. The percentage of Americans who believe the country is on the wrong track has long been alarmingly high. The 2016 presidential campaign, which began with much hope, concluded with the candidates of both major political parties disliked and distrusted. A *New York Times* / CBS poll the weekend before election day found that 83 percent of Americans were disgusted with the state of American politics. We are having a crisis of confidence in our ability to be self-governing.

This deep disappointment has moved the discourse in the two major political parties, Republicans and Democrats, further to the right and left, respectively. Moreover, the debate among adherents of the major political parties has grown decidedly harsh and personal. I often would get asked by my constituents about the state of civility in the country. Since I come from a military background, with a reputation as a straight shooter, they were curious about how I handled the acrimony. I confirmed my disappointment with the general discourse but was quick to add that this is ours to solve. This is a government "of the people, by the people, for the people," and if we don't like Congress and are unhappy with the state of politics and policy, *we the people* must change it.

There can be no doubt; we face serious challenges. They span the full spectrum of American life. How do we reform our tax code, regulatory process, and trade policies to facilitate economic growth so that everyone benefits? What must be done to better prepare our people to compete in the global economy? How do we reform mandatory spending programs to put them on a sustainable path for future generations? What must be done to strengthen our military and other aspects of national power so that we can protect our people and cherished way of life, and help promote order and stability in the world where American interests can flourish? How can we promote societal harmony here at home so that we maintain law and order, while also ensuring justice and equal opportunity for all? And among our most pressing issues, how do we come together as a people to address our budget deficit and begin to pay down the debt? This last question is especially important since issues of deficit and debt have been central to the decline and fall of all previous major republics. As Scottish philosopher David Hume once said, "A nation must destroy its debt, or the debt will destroy the nation."

From politics to policy, it is clear that our republic is in trouble. Yet in the face of the current crisis it is important to keep perspective and not lose faith. Our nation has faced serious troubles before. Times were tougher at Valley Forge and during the darkest days of the Depression, and even with regard to the deficit and debt, in relation to gross domestic product (GDP), we were in rougher shape immediately following World War II.

We have solved difficult problems in the past, and we still have the capacity to accomplish hard things today. We have the ability to bring our people together. In my life, I have seen the human condition under enormous stress, and while that has at times ended in heartbreak and failure, I've also seen what is possible with leadership. What we need now is *leadership*. We need leadership that identifies and explains our challenges in a manner that unifies and motivates us to act. That action must solve problems and improve the lives of everyday Americans. Finally, we need leadership that inspires us to believe—believe that we are still able to govern ourselves.

We need to believe in the republic. I still believe in the spirit of Philadelphia. Helping inspire all Americans to believe in our founding principles—our republic—to end this crisis of confidence is in large part the aim of this book. By overcoming our fears and keeping faith in our ability to be self-governing, we will find the strength and wisdom to enact the reforms necessary to revitalize the American dream.

My Life—Living the Dream

I certainly believe in the American dream, because I have lived it. I can't imagine any other place in the world where a kid from a working-class family would have so much opportunity. When I was growing up, our family didn't have a lot of money, but at home we did have love and discipline. That balance of love and discipline helped shape my character and set me on a path to becoming a contributing member of society, where I am fulfilling my responsibilities as a citizen in this republic.

I grew up in the 1970s, a different time from today. My parents, Bob and Barbara Gibson, were decent folks. My dad, a mechanic with Otis Elevator and member of the local Building and Construction Trades union, was a strict disciplinarian. I would tell my friends half-jokingly that he had a peculiar form of color blindness. He was not familiar with the color gray. Everything was black and white, and he always ensured that I knew what was expected of me and the difference between right and wrong. There were consequences too, sometimes severe, for getting the judgment wrong.

Mom's role was different. She emphasized love, always and unconditionally. She taught us the Golden Rule and led by example, focusing on the essential trait of empathy. Everyone was to be treated with dignity and respect—*everyone*. To the extent that I have been successful in politics, much credit goes to my mom. She had the ability to relate to all people, and I always admired that in her.

Mom was also remarkably resourceful and tough. We didn't need to hear the famous Bible story about the loaves and the fishes, because we saw it firsthand when Dad was laid off or on strike, which was often the case during the late 1970s. Mom was known throughout the neighborhood as "triple-coupon Barb." She would cut out those coupons from the Sunday paper and somehow make that work with just the union stipend for workers on strike or the unemployment check. She could really stretch a buck (during one of my congressional races, Mom did a commercial for us highlighting her incredible budgeting skills, so needed these days in Washington). It meant eating a lot of potpies (five for a dollar at Grand Union back then), but we ate. She also combined saintlike love with real toughness. Amazingly, she survived three bouts with cancer. After she defeated cancer for the third time in 2005, doctors told us they hadn't seen anything like it, to which my brother Bob proclaimed with dark Irish wit, "Mom is a tough woman to kill."

Years later, as I was writing this book, we lost Mom to her fourth bout with cancer. The woman who taught us so much about life in the end also showed us how to die. Unbeknownst to us, when Mom was informed she was sick again, she privately told our priest, Father George Fleming, that if it was her time, she was ready, but she felt obliged to fight. So fight she did. In her eightieth year and already weakened by oppressive chronic obstructive pulmonary disease that left her gasping for air, for over three weeks she endured the debilitating side effects of chemotherapy, while battling a large mass of lung cancer. Doctors put a knife through it, emplacing a stent to help her breathe, but in the end this all proved too much.

She struck a remarkable balance over those twenty-three days, between fighting the cancer tenaciously and treating everyone around her so graciously, including the doctors and nurses. When I fought in Iraq, I used to joke with my paratroopers that if I died on the battlefield, I hoped they'd find me with all my rifle magazines empty. I wanted to go out a fighter, firing every round I had in the process. Many years later, in November 2016 when we said goodbye to Mom, I realized where I got that from. Rest in peace, Mom.

Mom and me on Mother's Day.

The yin-and-yang parenting approach Mom and Dad used worked. My siblings, Kathleen, Bob, and Tim, and I understood what was expected of us and how important it was to be honest, trustworthy, hardworking, and kind. Growing up in a nine-hundred-square-foot ranch home on Williams Street in the historic village of Kinderhook (the hometown of our eighth president, Martin Van Buren) in Columbia County, upstate New York, this all seemed normal.

Although Dad liked to portray himself as the head of the

household, Mom knew how to get her way and get things done. After our youngest sibling, Tim, was born in December 1969, we became a family of six, making a nine-hundred-square-foot home, let's just say, challenging. One day my sister, Kathleen, was asked by our neighbor across the street, "Where is your brother Tim sleeping?" To which she innocently replied, "He sleeps next to the washing machine." (His bassinette was in the utility room.) Mom was mortified and Dad paid a price. When the spring came, she shamed him into building a three-hundred-square-foot addition onto our home. I was only five years old as this episode unfolded and couldn't fully appreciate the dynamic, but even then I could tell that Dad wasn't really calling the shots in our house. Mom was quiet but impressive, and I liked that.

Our parents instilled in us a strong work ethic. There were no allowances in our household—family chores were just part of the responsibility of growing up Gibson. If I wanted money, I had to earn it working outside the home. At the age of twelve, I started mowing neighbors' lawns, raking leaves, and shoveling snow to earn walking-around money. I came to realize I hated raking leaves. It seemed like every time I raked them into a neat pile, the wind would scatter them, forcing me to do it again. Later, in my thirties, I became aware that this wasn't just about leaves; it was a deeper issue. When I accomplish something, I don't like having it undone. Having that insight has made tackling life's challenges easier.

Anyway, by the time I was fourteen years old, I also had two paper routes, which gave me the experience of getting up early before school to deliver the *Albany Times Union*. I can't say that I enjoyed that, but it did begin to condition me for what came later in life in the military. At sixteen years old, I took a job mopping the floor and cleaning up the Village Hutte, a local diner in Kinderhook. The two things I remember most about that experience was how important standards were (I had to redo the floor a couple of times before internalizing that lesson) and that sometimes you have to deal with things you hate—in that case working in smoke-filled rooms. Both of my parents smoked and I never did.

The fall of my sixteenth year, I worked for Pete Chiaro at Yonder Farms in Kinderhook. To this day, he is a very successful small business owner. Back in 1980, he had a reputation as a hard boss, and on that score he did not disappoint. I was closely managed as I cleaned up and did odd jobs for him. Overall, that was a helpful experience for me, painful as it was to go through. Attention to detail matters.

After several years of these experiences, I was excited to join the Army National Guard the day after my seventeenth birthday, while still an eleventh grader, because I thought at least I wouldn't have to mow lawns and mop floors anymore. Then I experienced KP ("kitchen police") duty and grass-cutting detail in the military. It was an important life lesson—be careful about drawing hasty conclusions.

Still, my experience with "civilian jobs" was not complete. While at Siena College, I needed additional income to augment the National Guard pay and $100 ROTC stipend I was receiving, so I took a part-time job with KeyBank. I served as a clerk, filing paperwork and answering calls from checkout clerks in grocery stores across New York State who were experiencing problems with KeyBanks terminals (an early version of the ATM that was fielded in the 1980s). I would help them troubleshoot to get the terminals working again. I appreciated the experience and certainly needed the money. All of that income, in addition to max Pell grants and New York State tuition assistance, enabled me to graduate from college (the first ever in my family to do that) with only $8,000 of debt. Considering that my parents could not afford to provide anything toward my college, that's not much debt, even in 1986 dollars, and I was able to pay it off within seven years of serving in the Army.

All of these variegated experiences imbued in me a habit of working hard and saving money, what the Founders often described as thrift. That made it all the more painful to watch my dad spend so much time either laid off or on strike in the late 1970s. Those were not good days for our family. Dad seemed stripped of his dignity and often in a bad mood. My dad's pain and shame affected me. I was sad for him and embarrassed for our family.

I was rooting for him, but in some ways that made it worse. During the winter of 1977–78, when I was on the eighth-grade basketball team, Dad would pick up me and my friend Mark Zander after practice. After we got into the car, I would regularly ask him, "Did you get a job today?" I didn't realize how painful that was for Dad, to hear his son constantly asking if he had work, until Mom explained it to me. Evidently it bothered him so much that he asked Mom to talk to me about it. After listening to Mom, I realized that Dad's not being able to provide for his family hurt his pride and self-esteem. I stopped asking him and felt bad I ever did, but ever since I've been a big believer in the dignity of work.

I didn't fully realize it at the time, but the searing experience of Dad being out of work was also shaping my nascent political views. It was a period of mixed emotions. During the school day, I was with my friends and learning about this great country— especially the founding era and how we changed the course of world history. I was happy. Then I would come home and see Dad out of work and in a bad mood. A curious lad, I would turn on the TV to watch the news and see our president. He seemed like such a good person—a Naval Academy graduate, a straitlaced family man—but he talked to us as if our best days were behind us. When President Carter said we should lower our thermostats and our expectations, I just couldn't reconcile that with the great country I was learning about in history class.

My typical day back then was like an emotional roller coaster—happy, sad, confused. You could say I was in the space to be influenced by Ronald Reagan. I felt as if he were talking directly to me, and our home became like a scene right out of the 1980s sitcom *Family Ties*, with me playing the part of Alex Keaton. I said to Dad in the fall of 1980, "Ronald Reagan is our guy. You need to vote for him. He has a plan to get you back to work and to make our country strong again." Dad would have none of it. He voted for Jimmy Carter again in 1980. Sure, it was disappointing, but it was also a life lesson in politics. People don't always vote for what's in their best interest. As an interesting postscript, Dad did vote for Reagan in 1984, and generally voted for Republican presidential candidates for the rest of his life, although he never changed his party affiliation. He went to his grave a "Truman Democrat," as he described himself. As for me, I became the first Republican in our family, and it was Ronald Reagan who inspired it.

Probably the most defining moment in my young life came in failure. In high school, I was the centerfielder and co-captain of our varsity baseball team. As a junior, I batted .441 and led not only Ichabod Crane High School, but also the entire ten-team Patroon Conference. My star was on the rise. I received letters from colleges, recruiting me to attend their school. The one farthest away was Wittenberg University in Ohio. Part of the reason

I was the first in my family to go to college was because at the age of seventeen, my plan was to be centerfield for the New York Mets, and to do that I thought I needed to play college ball first.

Of course, I was never going to play for the Mets, but at that age you couldn't convince me otherwise. Ultimately I chose Siena College over the others to best position myself to be drafted into the pros. I was impressed that they had just had two of their players drafted the previous year. Siena was also a great Catholic institution in the Franciscan tradition, which made my parents proud, but I would be less than candid if I said that's why I chose them. It was baseball.

Anyway, after spending the summer following high school graduation at Fort Benning, Georgia, for Army Advanced Individual Training (I had spent the summer between my junior and senior years of high school at Basic Training, but there wasn't enough time to complete both basic and advanced training before school started, so troopers like me went through "split option," doing this comprehensive training requirement over a two-summer period), I reported for Siena baseball tryouts in late August 1982. I spent a couple of weeks practicing with the team and seemed to be doing fine but ultimately was cut from the roster. I was absolutely devastated. Even though, given my Army commitment, I was the only prospective player there who didn't play summer ball, which must have degraded my skills, I never saw it coming.

My dream was crushed. My first and only plan was to be a professional baseball player, and I had no backup. True, I was an enlisted man in the Army National Guard, but that was a part-time job I planned to keep while playing baseball. Now I had no plan and was still enrolled at a challenging college. I was only a low-B student during high school, and all indicators pointed to academic struggles ahead in college.

After about forty-eight hours of complete psychological dislocation, I made a decision to enroll in Army ROTC and become a regular Army officer after college. This was ironic, because only two weeks earlier I had turned down the ROTC officer trying to recruit me to join. I had thanked the officer for his interest in me, but I was enlisted and satisfied with that since I was going to play baseball. Then, after being cut, "hat in hand," I walked back in to the Quonset huts where Siena ROTC had barracks and asked them if they would take me.

Incredibly, all of this was happening in my life precisely when the movie *An Officer and a Gentleman* first came to the big screen. There is a scene in the movie when the young naval cadet, played by Richard Gere, is intensely hazed by the main drill sergeant, played by Lou Gossett Jr., and after completely breaking him down, Gossett asks Gere, "Why are you still here?" To which Gere responds, "Because I got no place else to go." I had just made the decision to join ROTC only twenty-four hours earlier and felt so uncomfortable sitting there in the movie theater, wondering if anyone else could tell how desperate I was, too.

Although there was no way of knowing it at the time, being cut from the baseball team ended up being the best thing that ever happened to me. For the first time, I got my priorities straight and excelled in academics. I earned a 3.7 GPA the first semester, and when I shared that with my former high school teachers, they were amazed. It only got better—straight 4.0 GPA from second-semester sophomore year on, graduating magna cum laude and the top history student in the class of 1986. I did all that in three and a half years, finishing a semester early.

I spent my last semester, the fall of 1985, at American University in the Washington Semester Program. This enabled me to hear directly from policymakers like members of Congress and administration officials and to get some experience with an internship in town. It was a wonderful opportunity that, as it turns out, several of my House colleagues also shared, including Speaker of the House Paul Ryan. It was a great capstone to my college experience.

None of that would have happened if I hadn't gotten cut from the baseball team—I'm sure of it. Had I played ball, I probably would have remained a low-B student at best and had a completely different path in life. This is truly an example of the line from the country song, "thank God for unanswered prayers."

———

Joining the military was the biggest break in my professional life. After finishing at Siena, I couldn't wait to get on active duty. Unfortunately, the Army was tracking a May graduation and planned to bring me on in August 1986. Realizing there would be a delay, the last thing I wanted to do was sit around. So I pursued a local job as I awaited orders.

In January 1986, I was hired by John Faso, a young professional who had moved to our village a couple of years earlier. He was the chief of the Legislative Bill Drafting Commission at the state capitol in Albany and gave me a position proofreading bills and running errands. John was a good boss and I appreciated the experience. In the small-world category, this past January, John replaced me in Congress.

My orders were eventually moved up and I reported for active duty the first week of March. I was an infantry officer and it was a hard life, but throughout, the Army was always very good to me and my family. Although I had to serve in combat to get it, the Army paid for my graduate school, which enabled me to earn a PhD in government at Cornell University, before teaching American politics for three years at the U.S. Military Academy at West Point, from

1995 to 1998. Years later, while I was earning War College credit, our family had the opportunity to live in California, near Mary Jo's sister and brother and their families. That was 2006–7, in between combat deployments to Iraq, and our family had a wonderful experience in the San Francisco Bay Area, as I served as a national security affairs fellow at the Hoover Institution at Stanford University. That rare opportunity enabled me to work closely with former U.S. attorney general and counselor to the president Ed Meese (we had initially met while I taught at West Point with Meese's son Mike) and to become friends with renowned historian Victor Davis Hanson, and receive mentorship from former secretary of state George Shultz and former secretary of defense Bill Perry. During that year at Stanford, I published my first book, *Securing the State*, on U.S. civil-military relations and national security decision making.

It was a tremendous privilege to serve and lead great soldiers. I learned and grew in all of these experiences. I saw some of the best our country had to offer serving in our ranks. What an incredible institution, the U.S. military. While our armed forces are not perfect, there is much to celebrate and revere about them. In a country that espouses the ideal of equal opportunity, the military is an institution that strengthens our political culture. There is only one color in the U.S. Army, and that is "Army Green." I served with people of every imaginable background in a system that was the most meritocratic I have witnessed in my life. I've been unquestionably shaped by these experiences, which helped a working-class kid rise to colonel in the U.S. Army and later serve in the Congress. That is truly an "only in America" story.

In my time in the Congress, I did everything I could to help restore faith in this exceptional way of life and in our ability to be self-governing. I served as a citizen legislator, self-imposing term limits on my time in the House and then following through on my pledge, leaving after six years. Recognizing the hard choices that I would have to make to help guide us back to a balanced budget, and knowing the importance of leading by example, my wife, Mary Jo, and I decided to voluntarily give our hard-earned military pension back to the taxpayers for the period we served in the Congress. We did not think it was right to "double dip" when we were asking others to do more with less for the sake of future generations. In the end, we voluntarily gave back over $300,000 to U.S. taxpayers, which represented more than our entire net worth. That has affected our family budget as we now pay for our children's college, but it was just plainly the right thing to do.

In Washington, D.C., I served on and made significant contributions to the House Armed Services, Agriculture, and Small Business Committees. I was also active in many issue areas and caucuses beyond those committees of jurisdiction, helping craft significant legislation that enhances opportunity and improves the human condition in this country. In the process, our family made many friendships with congressional families from both political parties. Mary Jo and I cherish those relationships still.

Contrary to conventional wisdom, there actually are lots of opportunities for members and their families on both sides of the aisle to socialize and get to know one another, and members get along much better than what's reported in the media. I played on the congressional baseball team one year and really enjoyed that experience. The annual baseball game is played for charity in the Washington Nationals Park in front of about ten thousand or so people. After aspiring to be a major-league baseball player earlier in life, it was awesome to get an at bat in an actual big-league park. In the fourth inning, when I reached first base on a walk, I looked up to Heaven and thought, "Dad [he had died in 2008], I reached base in a major-league stadium!... Okay, don't ask any questions." Seriously, that was an experience I never thought I would have after being cut from my Division I baseball team many moons ago. I also played on the congressional basketball team a couple of years. That was another charity event where I had fun and got to better know a number of my colleagues.

I was one of the hundred or so members who slept in their office. It made no sense for me to get an apartment in D.C. when I routinely worked at my office until 11:00 p.m. while in legislative session. Besides, since we were giving back our Army pension to the taxpayer, sleeping in my office was also a way to both stay focused on the job and save money for my family. The members who stayed in their offices saw each other every morning in the gym where we worked out, showered, and prepared for the day. These workouts provided another great opportunity to build strong bonds. I also shared meals with colleagues fairly regularly and with our spouses when they were in town. Finally, during congressional delegation trips within the United States and overseas, members had a prime opportunity to get better acquainted and find common ground.

All of these experiences helped me forge strong bipartisan friendships that facilitated getting things accomplished for my constituents. That's why we were there—to serve others and this nation. I left the institution with strong faith in the members and in the American people, convinced that we have the ability to revitalize our republic.

As a national leader, I also did my best to set a positive example as a citizen, which starts at home. Indeed, among all the important responsibilities I've had in my life—combat commander, West Point professor, congressman—by far the most important has been (and is) husband and father. With three teenagers, Katie (nineteen), Maggie (eighteen), and Connor (sixteen), this is still a work in progress for Mary Jo and me as our marriage moves into our third decade, but we are committed to doing our part to help shape and guide our children to be successful, responsible, and happy. The point here is that a strong republic begins with the citizen and the family. I have had a blessed life, living the American dream.

American Exceptionalism

As we survey the current political landscape and take inventory of the daunting challenges we face, we should also count our blessings. Sometimes it's hard to appreciate just how young we are as a country in comparison to the rest of the world. I had a moment of clarity on that score while sitting at a bar just outside of London on leave from the Berlin Brigade in April 1989. As the owner of the establishment passed me my second pint, he mentioned that his bar first opened in the fourteenth century. He showed some amusement when I responded, "That's incredible—your bar is older than my country!"

We are young, but we have the longest-standing constitution in the world. Two factors explain our longevity, political stability, and economic prosperity—our *constitutional arrangement* that diffuses power, protects liberty, and facilitates peaceful, evolutionary change, and our *unique political culture* that celebrates and advances the individual while valuing and balancing the needs of the community. That historical balance in our legal and cultural arrangements has enabled us to endure and flourish where other nations have struggled and perished.

It's clear—what our Founders established was truly exceptional.

Although far from perfect, our seminal documents (the Declaration of Independence, the Constitution, and the Bill of Rights) helped establish a framework that promotes civic virtue and facilitates a commitment to constant improvement toward the ideals professed in those documents. That is the spirit of Philadelphia.

———

Comparative analysis helps make the point. The American founding experience stands in stark contrast to that of its eighteenth-century contemporary, the French Revolution. What started in the late 1780s over debt and French king Louis XVI's unsuccessful attempt to extract more taxes from the masses to pay for it quickly led to major social and political turmoil and change.

In 1789, at the outset of the French Revolution, Parisians were proud of their actions in the name of "liberty, equality, and fraternity." However, because they never anchored their revolution with a constitutional arrangement to prevent tyrannical abuse of power, in just a few years they lost their republic in chaotic upheaval and widespread bloodshed. No matter what the leaders of the new French Republic did to enact change, nothing seemed to satisfy the most radical elements of the revolutionary cause, the so-called Jacobins, and their leader Maximilien Robespierre, who kept clamoring for more reform. Exasperated by the chaos, Parisians eventually put Robespierre in charge and gave him extraordinary powers to restore stability to the new political order. Just the opposite occurred. Robespierre abused power and launched what became known as the Reign of Terror. He considered a traitor anyone not fully supportive of the complete transformation of France and ordered mass detentions and summary executions. What started with so much promise ended violently. In the last words of French patriot Madame Jeanne-Marie Roland before mounting the guillotine on the Place de la Concorde in Paris at the height of the Reign of Terror, "O liberty! O liberty! What crimes have been committed in your name."

In the end, even Robespierre could not live up to the unrealistic expectations he helped established. A year later, he too was detained and sent to the guillotine. The French experiment with a republic died with him. The French people demanded a leader who could bring an end to the madness. They got it in the form of Napoleon Bonaparte, who seized and quickly consolidated power, ultimately becoming emperor. The lesson for the educated class in Europe was that the masses could not govern themselves.

The American case was not without passion, drama, and instability, but unlike in France, our republic survived and flourished. That stark difference in outcome warrants further examination. As with the French, liberty was a founding principle for us. Although we did not put a marker down for equality as the French did, we did advance strong arguments for *equal opportunity* and a *flourishing life*. The Declaration of Independence was a bold and optimistic statement on human potential:

> We hold these truths to be self-evident, that all men are created equal, that they are endowed by their Creator with certain unalienable rights, that among these are life, liberty and the pursuit of happiness.—That to secure these rights, governments are instituted among men, deriving their just powers from the consent of the governed.

This was a truly radical statement. The very notion that sovereignty started with the individual and that ordinary people could govern themselves was unheard of in the eighteenth century. After all, that was the era of the "divine right of kings." This political theory dates back to Roman emperor Constantine in the early fourth century AD, and was later strengthened by Holy Roman Emperor Charlemagne in AD 800. It posited that God explicitly empowered certain individuals to rule over men to bring order and Christianity to the world.

The pope in Rome, and later Protestant leaders as well, played essential roles in legitimizing rulers. Thus this political theory joined the monarchy and the church, centralizing power controlling the people. The masses, according to this political design, benefited with security in this life and salvation in the next. The expectation in this arrangement was that kings and queens cared for their people, with a certain historical smile bestowed on benevolent monarchs. However, there were few guarantees for the rights and well-being of people of the realm, Magna Carta excepting, and monarchs could and often did rationalize their harsh policies on security exigencies. Moreover, the burden to finance this entire enterprise fell on the people, or serfs. People with wealth—the members of the aristocracy—generally paid no taxes. These injustices eventually sowed the seeds of political instability and revolution in the eighteenth century, including our own.

Still, influential philosophers over the centuries provided political justification for the divine right. Writing in the seventeenth century, English philosopher Thomas Hobbes in *Leviathan* argued that this monarchical political system was necessary to prevent widespread civil war in a reality that was "nasty, brutish, and short." Change occurred, albeit slowly. Later in that century, John Locke introduced the concept of political legitimacy in which a monarch's just powers derived from the consent of the governed—a significant development in the history of ideas. A scientist and philosopher who put a premium on learning from experience and elevating the individual, Locke would figure prominently in our founding philosophy. Roughly half a century later, European philosopher Jean-Jacques Rousseau introduced the notion of the "general will" (a supposition made by the national leader of what constituted the greater good) as essential to political legitimacy and justifying political action. Rousseau's vision centering on the community stood in stark contrast to Locke's, which focused on the individual. Indeed, Rousseau's complete subordination of the individual's interests to community interests later factored into, and to some degree rationalized, Robespierre's Reign of Terror. However, in America the influences of Locke and Rousseau collided, resulting in a leavening of their most pungent political effects, and unlike in Europe, we developed a unique hybrid, a more balanced political culture that contributed to our political stability and economic success.

French philosopher Charles-Louis Montesquieu, writing around the same time as Rousseau, also had a major influence on the American Founders. In *The Spirit of Laws*, Montesquieu theorized on constitutional arrangements to prevent the accumulation and abuse of power. He advanced the concept of the separation of powers between the executive, legislative, and judicial branches. The independent judiciary was a novel concept in the history of ideas. Up to that point, judges had been an extension of the monarch.

While Montesquieu's original contributions were real and profound, he was influenced by earlier philosophers. Socrates, Plato, Aristotle, and Cicero all articulated various forms of separation of powers. In Plato's *Republic*, the author expounded on the topics of power and justice. He established that throughout history patterns emerge in which regimes proceed through an inexorable cycle of revolution, solidification, and decay, eventually leading to another round of violent upheaval as the dynamic repeats itself. To escape this dialectic, Plato theorized that power must be arrayed in a countervailing manner to prevent accumulation and tyrannical abuse, and that such juxtaposition would produce political stability. For him, this was "the one, the few, and the many" (an executive, a legislature, and the people).

Although they had many fundamental differences, his pupil Aristotle generally agreed with Plato on this point. Aristotle further developed his political theory in one of his major works, *Politics*, where he provided extensive comparative analysis of constitutions. It was there that he noted the importance of reining in and balancing political power.

Later Roman philosopher Cicero advanced his own version of the separation of powers. By balancing power between the consuls, the Senate, and the people, the Roman Republic could be preserved. Yet in Cicero's time that power relationship went out of balance. It started with the rise of Julius Caesar to one of the consul positions. When he crossed the Rubicon River to attack forces loyal to the Senate, he set in motion a series of violent events that brought about the end of the republic. After briefly consolidating power, Julius was murdered by Brutus and Cassius, but this did not lead to the restoration of liberty-minded peace as these conspirators had intended. Instead it led to more violence and instability. Ultimately, weighed down by serious financial debt and exhausted by constant conflict, the citizens of Rome sought stability. They got it in the form of the first Roman emperor, Caesar Augustus. In a stroke of political genius, Augustus elevated the memory of Cicero (who had also died a violent death in the struggles) to the role of philosopher of Rome. By doing so, he cast the new political arrangement as the continuance of the republic, but this could not hide the fact that a new era had dawned. The republic was gone for good.

The Founders were conscious of all this history. Indeed, George Washington's favorite play was *Cato*, a theatrical performance of Roman republican virtue. Our Founders fused principles of liberty and self-governance along with a constitutional arrangement (the separation of powers) to preserve it. The citizen of this new republic was markedly different from the "subject" of the crown. The citizen had rights *and* responsibilities and played an instrumental role in governance and all facets of life.

The heads of state in Europe scoffed at this radical political experiment in America and believed it would never work. No collection of mostly farmers could ever successfully govern themselves. Chaos would ensue, and eventually, as later in France, the Americans would beg for the return of the monarchy to restore order.

Except that never happened. Decades later, perplexed at America's success, leaders in France summoned the smartest person they knew to go to America to find out why. His name was Alexis de Tocqueville, and he spent close to a year in the United States before writing *Democracy in America*. His report clearly disappointed the European monarchs. Tocqueville found the United States to be flourishing, and he cited two reasons. First, the constitutional arrangement empowered the citizen and prevented the accumulation and abuse of government power. Second, America appeared to be forging a new political culture that balanced economic freedom with strong bonds of civic obligation fulfilled through faith-based and volunteer organizations. Tocqueville believed that those unique arrangements and characteristics would generate significant national strength in the future. In time, the world would be forced to respect American exceptionalism.

Liberty and Chaos

It wasn't so clear at the outset, however, that we would survive and flourish. Our country struggled under its initial political arrangement, the Articles of Confederation.

The Articles empowered the original thirteen states. But it soon became apparent that this arrangement created internecine competition and chaotic relations among the states. Some of the states, looking to gain economic advantage, pursued independent trade negotiations with foreign nations. States also started making their own money, which made interstate commerce more challenging.

The new federal Congress under the Articles of Confederation lacked the power to tax, and that created major problems. First, without the ability to raise revenues, the country struggled to pay off its Revolutionary War debt, which hurt our credit standing with other nations. Questionable credit adversely impacted U.S. exports, which slowed the nation's economy. Without revenues, we also couldn't pay the soldiers who had bravely fought to win our independence. This caused widespread disenchantment in the ranks. Since soldiers had bills to pay too, not being paid for their service also made debtors of them. The same went for the farmers who had supported the Revolution with their crops and livestock. At that point we were largely a nation of debtors.

When some of the states enacted new taxes to raise revenues to send to the federal government to help pay off the war debt, it caused turmoil. Farmers who could not afford to pay the taxes lost their farms in foreclosure proceedings, prompting a fierce popular backlash. Uprisings occurred frequently in those early years, including the infamous Shays' Rebellion in Massachusetts in 1786. Across the land, debtors' prisons filled up. For a nation founded upon the principle of liberty, we were off to a rough start, and the irony was rich, considering that the American Revolution had been inspired in part by a tax revolt.

Our national leaders quickly realized that we were having significant problems under the Articles of Confederation. They met several times in those first few years to attempt to gain consensus on how to amend them. After yet another such effort in Annapolis in 1786 ended in failure, leading American statesmen sensed that something more ambitious had to be done. The economy was struggling. Farms were foreclosing. Law and order was deteriorating. We had liberty, but we also had chaos. The country was faltering and needed a new direction. Invitations went out to the states to send delegates to a convention in Philadelphia the following spring, and there was hope that decisive change was on the horizon.

Toward a More Perfect Union

The delegates met in May 1787 and went to work. Change is always hard. The delegates were painfully aware of the previous failures to amend the Articles. Recognizing that, and believing that national panic could ensue if their daily deliberations were reported in the press, they agreed to keep the proceedings secret. Next, rather boldly, they resolved to draft an entirely new constitution to replace the Articles of Confederation. The delegates knew that this would be controversial, since the Continental Congress provided no such authority. The delegates were only authorized to bring forward recommendations amending the Articles.

The debate at the convention was wide-ranging and often intense. There were strong voices for liberty, including a few who were not comfortable scrapping the Articles of Confederation. Some of the strongest supporters of the Articles stayed home. For example, Patrick Henry declined to attend because he "smelled a rat." On the other end of the spectrum, Alexander Hamilton believed a major overhaul of the governmental structure was necessary to provide order and stability and to promote economic prosperity. Hamilton argued for a strong presidential system, which most delegates opposed.

Eventually the discussions took the form of detailed plans. Delegates from New Jersey and Virginia had dueling frameworks. Naturally, Virginia wanted a system that favored the most populous states, such as theirs. Edmund Randolph offered their plan. New Jersey sought to keep the loci of power within the states and allocated regardless of population size. William Paterson offered that plan. Neither, however, gained a majority of support, and the convention gridlocked until a compromise proposal, offered by Roger Sherman of Connecticut, rallied it. After considerable debate, the convention adopted Sherman's "Connecticut compromise." It featured a bicameral legislature, with a House of Representatives based on population size, and a Senate to which each state legislature sent two individuals.

This agreement was a turning point for the convention. After much strife, both large and small states felt they had secured key concessions, and an air of compromise swept over the convention, providing a constructive environment for the remaining issues to be decided. Among those concerns, crafting the powers of the executive branch was the most controversial.

With the memory of King George's despotic rule fresh and painful, nearly all of the delegates feared a strong executive (Hamilton was a notable exception). Most of the delegates were conflicted on how to proceed. On the one hand, they did not want to vest too much power in the executive branch; on the other, they knew that the absence of executive power was a major deficiency of the Articles of Confederation, and the biggest reason why the U.S. government lacked the respect of other nations around the world. Under the Articles, executive functions were performed by congressional leaders, which most delegates believed was not working well, for a variety of reasons. Ultimately they chose a singular executive (they considered a plural) and made it coequal with the legislative and judicial branches. In doing so they fully embraced Montesquieu's separation-of-powers design.

The Constitution was not only the product of compromise, it was also designed to drive peaceful, evolutionary change through a *process of compromise.* I frequently made this point with my colleagues and constituents. In fact, in the spring of 2015, I hosted a book club for some of my constituents to highlight this point. We read and discussed Edward J. Larson's *A Magnificent Catastrophe*, a thoughtful book about the founding era and the presidential election of 1800. That election, between incumbent John Adams, a Federalist, and Thomas Jefferson, a Democrat-Republican, took more than thirty ballots in the House of Representatives to resolve before Jefferson was declared the winner. It also marked the first time we peacefully transferred power from one political party to another.

There is a perception among some of my Tea Party Patriot friends that the founding era was perfect and the Founders were demigods without fault who never compromised, and if only present-day leaders were like them, all would be well in the universe. I revere our history and the Founders (and my Tea Party friends), but see all of this in perspective. Our Founders were human and struggled mightily to solve the issues of the day. Under the most trying circumstances, they succeeded, which makes me admire them all the more. During the book club discussion, my constituents were surprised at how many problems the Founders struggled with that we still deal with today, such as when to compromise, concerns over debt, matters of war and peace, and religion in politics. That evening was both enjoyable and productive, because as they left our home, I felt that my constituents better appreciated our history and my work in Congress.

———

As the delegates departed Philadelphia, they knew that the dramatic nature of the proposed changes would cause their countrymen anxiety. To help make the case for such bold change, the Founders presented a succinct, compelling argument. We know it today as the Preamble to the Constitution:

> We the people of the United States, in order to form a more perfect union, establish justice, insure domestic tranquility, provide for the common defense, promote the general welfare, and secure the blessings of liberty to ourselves and our posterity, do ordain and establish this Constitution for the United States of America.

Before they adjourned, the delegates decided that when nine of the thirteen states ratified the new Constitution, it would go into effect. Among all the ambitious new concepts and stipulations, arguably this was the most controversial. First, as previously mentioned, there was no authority to discard the Articles of Confederation. Second, and most significantly, according to the Articles, any changes to that document *required the approval of all thirteen states*. That stipulation alone left the new Constitution vulnerable to legal challenge. However, as vigorous as opposition was, no serious effort to defeat the Constitution on the grounds of legal standing emerged.

Instead, opponents of the Constitution focused their criticisms on the substance of the proposed reforms. Patrick Henry was the most vocal and led the effort to defeat ratification at Virginia's convention. Across the country, letters to the editor and other opinion pieces in widely circulated pamphlets became the battleground where those for and against the Constitution presented their arguments. In my home state of New York, all early indicators pointed to its defeat. The election to seat delegates to New York's ratifying convention produced a majority pledged to oppose it. As in Virginia, leaders in New York preferred the status quo, which provided them with considerable influence and power. For the masses in those states, the Articles preserved liberty. Farmers in New York hated the idea that after a long, hard struggle to win their liberty, they would have to be governed by a strong central power far from New York. They expected their delegates in Poughkeepsie to save them from such a fate.

Recognizing the formidable opposition that was organizing, proponents of the Constitution took action. To help improve the chances of its ratification, James Madison, Alexander Hamilton, and John Jay collaborated in writing a series of opinion pieces to persuade state delegates to support the Constitution. These pieces, subsequently published together as the *Federalist Papers*, addressed the major arguments against ratification. Among the most formidable was overcoming conventional wisdom regarding the optimal size of a republic. Since Aristotle, philosophers had maintained that only by keeping a republic small and homogeneous could it survive the inevitable forces of fragmentation and disintegration caused by "faction," or what we commonly call today "special interests." As late as the mid-1700s, philosophers were still reinforcing that claim.

The principal author of the Constitution, James Madison,

acknowledged the dangers of faction but offered a decidedly different way of dealing with it. He maintained that it was better to control the effects than to try to cure it, which would encroach upon liberty. Instead, in *Federalist* no. 10, Madison argued for "extending the sphere" so that the multitude of groups would naturally check each other through extensive competition. Later, in *Federalist* no. 51, Madison bolstered this argument with a sober commentary on human nature and the need for countervailing forces as a check against the human tendency to abuse power:

> Ambition must be made to counteract ambition.... If men were angels, no government would be necessary. If angels were to govern men, neither external nor internal controls on government would be necessary. In framing a government which is to be administered by men over men, the great difficulty lies in this: You must first enable the government to control the governed; and in the next place, oblige it to control itself.

It was a masterful argument to convince a people who coveted liberty to agree to more centralized power in the national government. Madison's point was essentially that in order to protect and preserve liberty, we needed to do better than the Articles of Confederation. We needed the Constitution so we could both govern ourselves and prevent tyranny.

It worked. One by one, starting with Delaware in December 1787, states ratified the Constitution. Ten months later, New Hampshire became the ninth state to do so, and it officially went into effect. This left the states opposed, like New York, in a quandary. The people of the state expected their delegates to defeat ratification, but then New York would be left outside of the

Union to fend for itself, which made no sense to the delegates. In the end, New York ratified the document, but only after joining several other states asking for amendments, including the Bill of Rights.

The Bill of Rights was subsequently ratified in December 1791, marking a major milestone in the history of ideas. This solidified the American founding as a new era of liberty and self-governance. These amendments were grounded in the reality of past abuses.

Reacting to King George's suppression of liberties, the First Amendment protects freedoms of speech, religion, press, assembly, and the right to petition government to redress grievances. In response to the king's soldiers marching on our guns and ammunition, actions that had led to armed resistance at Lexington and Concord in April 1775, starting the Revolution, the Second Amendment ensures that law-abiding citizens have the right to keep and bear arms. Never again would the government be allowed to take our guns without due process of law.

Reacting to King George's orders for his troops to be housed in our homes without our consent and searching our belongings without warrant, we enacted the Third and Fourth Amendments outlining the steps that had to be taken to lawfully quarter troops and the due process requirements before government officials could search our premises and property. The Fifth Amendment further protected our life and property, making clear that we couldn't be forced to be a witness against ourselves and what steps the government must follow before taking property for public use. The Sixth, Seventh, and Eighth Amendments provided constitutional protections for those accused of crimes, including the right to counsel, to know the charges and witnesses against us, that any trial would be public and speedy, that we would not face trial twice for the same crime, and that we would be protected from torture. The Ninth and Tenth Amendments provided additional assurances to our commitment to limited government, stipulating that those powers not enumerated to the federal government were reserved to the states or the people.

The enactment of our Bill of Rights may be the brightest moment in the history of world freedom. It put true meaning and value to the term "empowered citizen." Taken together with the original document, that constitutional arrangement was at once idealistic and realistic. A government of the people was possible, but checks would be necessary. This came from a sober understanding of human nature and a close reading of history. Perhaps most inspired is the way this constitutional arrangement was forward-looking, anticipating changes in technology, societal norms, and the fortunes of peoples and governments. That has been essential to American success.

Forging the American Political Culture

American life during the founding era was a balance between individual and community, a blend that helped produce success *and* happiness. This is a story of the philosophical clash between the Enlightenment and the early Romantic period, and especially the works of Locke and Rousseau. The founding helped forge a political culture that was Locke (capitalism) by day and Rousseau (family and community) by night. This produced freedom and prosperity for individuals, who then shared with family, friends, and those in need in the community.

It starts with Locke, the Enlightenment, and capitalism. In accordance with our founding principles, individuals were free and with their liberty pursued their best interests, or utility. This approach allows people to live to their God-given potential. Capitalists play an essential role, taking on significant risk with their money to create business enterprises that produce goods and services. In the process, they hire workers to make the goods and services, with wages decided in the labor market. This capitalistic system, based on freedom and individuals selfishly pursuing their best interests, elevated those who heretofore had experienced no upward mobility.

Rousseau questioned the entire capitalistic enterprise and the underlying assumptions of the Enlightenment. He challenged conventional thinking on utility and freedom. On utility, he emphasized the complex nature of human psychology and that as humans our decisions and interactions are not easily reduced to mathematical equations where we can solve for x. We have a *soul* and we have emotions that sometimes override rational decision making. Enlightenment philosophers were troubled by these arguments because they were based on factors beyond perception and measurement. On freedom, Rousseau argued that our obligations to others made separating our interests from others' problematic. He harkened us to work toward the greater good of society.

Although there was never a moment in time that historians can point to and declare that we consciously did so, American political culture absorbed both of these differing viewpoints. In the process, we produced a new and unique way of living and interacting with each other. At the founding, we at once embraced laissez-faire capitalism and a strong sense of duty and commitment to our family and neighbors, behavior that at times translated to Americans making decisions against their own self-interest.

We were different from the peoples of Europe, who for hundreds of years lived under the all-powerful alliance between crown and church. European political culture was based on hierarchy, highly stratified, with no hope of upward mobility. As esteemed historian Louis Hartz argued, the United States had no such history and was "born free" to empower people to reach their potential. Accordingly, American political culture since the beginning has produced a more pragmatic people, willing to experiment so long as ideas stay within the lines of founding principles. Before Hartz, Tocqueville also noted the unique political culture of America in which the empowered citizens pursued their own interests, but in times of need joined with neighbors in the community to provide support. When a farmer lost a barn, neighbors gathered to help raise a new one, and there were volunteer organizations to support the individual and make communities stronger.

As Americans, the impulse to share and to sacrifice for the sake of others is woven into our social fabric as much as is acting in our best interests. That founding tradition of service to others lives on to this day in our Elks, Lions, Moose, Knights of Columbus, and Masons, as well as many other veterans' and faith-based organizations.

Rousseau influenced us to rebel against mere materiality and to respect ourselves by appreciating the mystery of the soul. You won't find an equation that helps you understand your emotions. There isn't a manual that informs you who to love, what you are passionate about, and what you despise. You choose these things by better understanding yourself—by allowing yourself to live free, trying new things, and occasionally getting out of your comfort zone.

Indeed, Rousseau provided a check against radical empiricism, and we are better off for it, providing of course that there are checks and balances to those impulses as well. Too many families have seen what happens to the "wild child" who never heeds caution and goes to excess on all things. That generally doesn't end well. Further, the French Revolution and the German

Third Reich were heavy on Rousseau's influence, subordinating the individual. That didn't end well either. The point is, we need balance.

At the founding, we had a political culture that balanced the needs of the individual and community and the impulses of materiality and spirituality. This approach often produced pragmatic politics, and that, along with our unique constitutional arrangement, facilitated political stability and the most freedom and prosperity the world has ever seen.

Losing Our Way—The Erosion of the Founding Principles

Beginning in the second half of the twentieth century, gradual changes to our constitutional arrangement and political culture have restricted our liberty, undermined confidence in our ability to be self-governing, fomented uncertainty in the economy, and contributed to poor policy decisions that have fueled fiscal and moral decay. This was not the result of any single decision. It was a series of policy choices and changes in norms over time that consolidated power in the executive branch and disrupted the delicate balance in our political culture, elevating the desires of the individual over the obligations to family, friends, and neighbors.

Over the course of world history, war, and the threat of it, has often made a casualty of liberty. That is part of the story here. With the emergence of the Soviet Union as a superpower and existential threat, we created massive bureaucracies to help the president exercise newly delegated powers to keep us safe. In the process, we significantly altered the legislative-executive branch relationship. Congress was a willing participant to these changes, enacting laws to transfer more power to the executive branch.

The National Security Act of 1947 consolidated several executive departments to create the Department of Defense and the Central Intelligence Agency. This was done to enhance national security—the first function of government. The problem in design, however, was that this massive expansion of government seriously degraded the Congress's ability to properly oversee the new entities. The act also established the precedent that largely unchecked consolidated executive power was necessary to address significant, complex problems.

During World War II we had done things differently. Congress played a key role in supervising wartime production. Indeed, this was how Senator Harry Truman made his reputation. Truman led the effort to fight fraud, waste, and abuse by unscrupulous business vendors during the war. His oversight hearings were legendary for their piercing criticism and effective efforts to enhance transparency and accountability. As a result, Truman, a decorated World War I hero, gained in national stature, catching the attention of President Franklin D. Roosevelt, who made him his vice presidential running mate in 1944.

Things changed after the National Security Act. The law established a new standard, with the secretary of defense and other political appointees taking up responsibilities that heretofore had been exercised by Congress. This was done despite explicit language in the Constitution directing that the people's representatives retain such authority. In Article I, Section 8 of the Constitution, Congress's responsibilities in developing and supervising the armed forces were:

> To raise and support armies, but no appropriation of money to that use shall be for a longer term than two years; To provide and maintain a navy; To make rules for the government and regulation of the land and naval forces; To provide for

calling forth the militia to execute the laws of the union, suppress insurrections and repel invasions; To provide for organizing, arming, and disciplining, the militia, and for governing such part of them as may be employed in the service of the United States, reserving to the states respectively, the appointment of the officers, and the authority of training the militia according to the discipline prescribed by Congress.

The Truman administration used this new law to confront the communist challenge. An internal document—National Security Council Memorandum 68 (NSC 68), written in 1950—provided the blueprint. It was far-reaching in scope, providing philosophical argument and strategic guidance for coherent, integrated action impacting all facets of American life. That the U.S. government was taking such action to deter the Soviets was not controversial or unwise. Previously, however, Congress would have played an instrumental role in providing planning guidance and enacting policies, and then during implementation the legislative branch would have had plenty of oversight mechanisms in place to track executive branch compliance. With the Cold War, we moved most of these responsibilities to the executive branch, and the legislative branch became more of a rubber stamp, a weak partner at best. These trends continue today, and it has been hard for Congress to reverse it.

The power transfer to the executive branch occurred in domestic policy too. President Lyndon B. Johnson, despite being the former Senate majority leader and cognizant of the critical role the legislative branch plays in the Founders' vision of separated powers, played a pivotal role in the further consolidation of executive powers. He proved especially adroit at using them, too. With the Great Society program, enacted by Congress, new bureaucracies were created with broad powers to promulgate rules affecting all dimensions of American life. This provided the executive branch with de facto legislative authorities in direct violation of the Constitution, which reserves those responsibilities for the people's representatives.

These trends continued under both Republican and Democratic administrations. For example, during the George W. Bush administration, the Patriot Act and the No Child Left Behind Act (NCLB) were signed into law, significantly expanding federal, executive-branch power. I opposed them both and voted against the reauthorization of the Patriot Act when it came up for a vote in 2011, because two provisions in it are unconstitutional. First, the "roving wiretap" section lowers the threshold for issuing warrants from specificity in person, place, and time (as required by the Fourth Amendment) to a general description. Second, Section 215 of the act (concerning business records) is drafted so broadly that it can be used to collect information on Americans without a warrant. Indeed, this was the section of the Patriot Act that provided authority for the U.S. government to collect metadata on all Americans. The Patriot Act continues the trend of transferring expansive, opaque, and unaccountable power from the legislative to the executive branch. It directly threatens the liberty of our citizens.

Similarly, NCLB overfederalized education policy, taking power away from local school districts and states and consolidating much of it in the unelected and unaccountable federal bureaucracy—the U.S. Department of Education. Moreover, the act relied heavily on unfunded mandates (in essence, the federal government directs action, but local governments have to figure out how to pay for it) and onerous high-stakes testing to compel states toward homogenized lesson plans. In my home state of New

York, such plans were hastily developed, robbing our classrooms of teacher creativity.

The Obama administration promulgated more bureaucratic rules and regulations than any previous administration. As a Congress, we defeated some of the worst ones. At one point the administration published a draft rule stipulating that spilled milk would be treated like spilled oil. This would have required our dairy farmers to invest tens of thousands of dollars in hazardous waste mitigation when life for them is already challenging enough. We can all agree that spilled milk is not a good thing, but good grief, let's be reasonable—not everything is a federal case. Many of us from both sides of the aisle protested, and the Obama administration ultimately withdrew the proposed rule.

We appreciated that, but it wasn't long afterward that they were back at it. About a year later the administration issued a draft rule that would have effectively banned children under the age of sixteen years of age from working on farms. My farmers were irate. For children of farmers, doing chores on the family farm is part of growing up in rural America. With bipartisan opposition in Congress, the administration withdrew that proposed rule too. However, for each unhelpful and wrongheaded rule we were able to defeat, many more got through, and they have had a painful impact on family-owned businesses across the country. We all know we need a regulatory state to promote health, safety, and justice, but many of these rules defy common sense. Bureaucratic rule-making must be reined in and Congress must reclaim its legislative responsibilities.

On the legislative front, the Obama administration accelerated the trend of expanding the federal government and consolidating power in the executive branch. The Dodd-Frank Act is just one example. It was intended to address the Wall Street meltdown of 2008 by holding the big banks accountable and ending the de facto policy of "too big to fail." It had the opposite effect. Overly aggressive bureaucratic rule-making made possible by that law has devastated our community banks, which had absolutely nothing to do with the Wall Street crash in 2008.

Dodd-Frank continues to hamper small businesses on Main Streets across America. In my congressional district, the expansion plan of one of our family-owned ski resorts was stymied by it. This business had an effective working relationship with a local community bank and had never had a previous issue getting credit or paying back their loans. In 2013 they made plans to build condominiums to expand lodging at their ski resort. It would have created jobs and produced more revenue for local government. But the deal could not get done because the size of the loan exceeded the Dodd-Frank limit and thus required a third entity (another bank or underwriter) to gain approval. We count on our community banks to extend credit to our small business owners, and that has been impeded by Dodd-Frank.

Changes in our constitutional arrangement have moved us far from the original design of the separation of powers. The Founders anticipated institutional jousting and occasional power grabs and believed that when that overreach by one branch occurred, the other two would assert themselves to restore proper balance. Complicating matters is that the legislative branch has willingly given away power to the executive branch, leaving the responsibility of preserving original intent with the judicial branch.

The U.S. Supreme Court's record on preserving the separation of powers has been mixed. When Franklin D. Roosevelt significantly expanded executive branch power (with congressional consent) in his first term, the Court initially balked. The *Schechter* decision (1935) found the first New Deal unconstitutional on the grounds that it overdelegated powers from the legislative to the executive branch. Things changed in his second term. After his landslide reelection in 1936, FDR challenged the Court. He proposed the Judicial Procedures Reform Bill of 1937, legislation that would add a new judge to the Supreme Court for every presiding judge over the age of seventy years and six months. Members of Congress from both parties saw through this as an attempt to intimidate the Supreme Court justices. Unfortunately, on that score it worked. Under pressure, the Court reversed its view on legislative delegation and rendered judgments supportive of FDR's expansion of executive action. These judicial decisions in the late 1930s cleared the way for a major transformation of the political landscape in the second half of the twentieth century.

Recently, however, the courts have reasserted themselves. On three separate occasions over the past couple of years, courts have issued injunctions against proposed Obama administration rules. These cases involved executive overreach in proposed Army Corps of Engineers and EPA jurisdiction expansion concerning "navigable waters," an executive-branch-imposed "cap and trade" scheme on greenhouse gas emissions, and executive amnesty for undocumented immigrants. In all three cases, the courts held that these actions overstepped executive authority—legislative powers reside with the Congress. Moreover, as this book goes to print, the courts have issued an injunction against the Trump administration's travel ban. It's encouraging to see the judicial branch reasserting itself as a separate and equal branch of government. I hope this trend continues.

Where is this all heading? During the Obama years, Republicans in Congress (including myself) were very critical of executive overreach. Now that we have a Republican administration, will they continue to insist on restoring legislative powers as outlined in the Constitution, or will they drop that priority out of political expediency? Will the Trump administration work with the Congress to restore proper balance to the separation of powers and strengthen the Constitution and rule of law, or will it continue the disturbing trend of consolidating executive-branch power and sidestepping the legislative process with expanded rule-making and overreliance on executive orders? Early indications are not reassuring on that score.

The right answer is to stand with the people and the Constitution. When we weaken the Congress, we take power away from the people, encroaching on liberty. By constitutional design, legislators work directly for the people, write the nation's laws, supervise the executive branch, and are accountable to the voters every two years. The president is the chief executive, carrying out the laws and administering the U.S. government, and is elected every four years.

The consolidation of power in the executive branch has encroached on freedoms and weakened due process of law, threatening many of the liberties protected in the Bill of Rights. With the rise of the "imperial presidency," the federal government has expanded its powers to surveil American citizens without warrant, and presidents from both political parties have taken us to war without the consent of the governed. The Founders explicitly gave those powers to the legislative branch because King George abused them when they were subjects under the crown. The Founders agreed with Montesquieu that the only way to prevent tyrannical abuse of power was to establish checks and balances through the separation of powers. Reform is necessary to restore balance.

As with constitutional arrangements, American political culture has also shifted since the mid-twentieth century. Our exceptionalism has faded to a degree, and we look more like Europe. We've discarded our balanced founding-era political culture and replaced it with more of a European statist model in which the citizen is eclipsed by the ever-expanding federal bureaucracy. Moreover, as *New York Times* columnist David Brooks found in his book *The Road to Character*, this period also witnessed the elevation of the individual over familial and community obligations, with more focus on materiality and the here and now.

These changes have affected our politics and policies, tending toward governmental excess and fiscal and moral decay. We have left behind the virtues that came with a blended political culture combining the best of Locke and Rousseau, forsaking it for German idealism—the new American philosophical guidepost.

German idealism spans the last decades of the eighteenth century and the first half of the nineteenth, and includes contributions from several very influential philosophers, including Kant, Reinhold, Fichte, and Hegel. A close reading of their works produces highly nuanced interpretations and enormous contributions across the full spectrum of philosophy. My intent here is not to trivialize the complexity of this school of thought or to libel it, but to point out how influential it's been in altering our political culture, especially Hegel's contributions. Hegel was critical of man's ability to be self-governing and placed great hope in an all-powerful state. In the powerful state, man could be perfected and the plight of people could be lifted.

I've always found it a shame that Europe never gave man a chance. After centuries of iron-fisted rule by monarchs, once free, Europe turned quickly to utopian schemes—empowered bureaucratic states, fascism, and communism—to address public problems and the unfairness in life. They never gave liberty an opportunity.

Our Founders made a conscious choice to do otherwise. Madison contemplated such utopian notions but ultimately rejected them, believing that the "cure would be worse than the disease." We put our belief in man, fallible as he was—and empowered the citizen. At the same time, Madison was not a fool. He knew the history of mankind was replete with treacherous individuals who seized power and ruled tyrannically. To safeguard against that, the Founders established checks and balances to prevent man from abusing us. In the mid-twentieth century, however, we started giving up on man, slouching toward collective schemes.

Progressives first brought Hegel to America and immediately challenged the laissez-faire approach to political life. Republican president Theodore Roosevelt was the bridge. He initially led the Progressive movement, but his focus was decidedly different from that of his successor, Democratic president Woodrow Wilson. Roosevelt sought to use the power of government as a referee to ensure that individuals could compete fairly. He was the first to employ fully the Sherman Antitrust Act of 1890 to bust up trusts and combinations, which were rigging the system for powerful monopolies at the expense of the individual small business owner and consumers. He also sought to protect consumers from the abuses of industry, restoring faith in the meatpacking industry. His focus was on ensuring fair competition so that man could flourish on his own.

The trajectory of the Progressive movement changed significantly with President Wilson, who gave it a decidedly statist bent, more in the spirit of Hegel. He significantly expanded the federal government's powers. Wilson's influence was considerable. Among many other actions, he convinced Congress to enact the Federal Reserve Act, which has forever changed monetary policy in this country by ensuring that the government and the banking industry have the power to regulate the economy in ways heretofore unimaginable. However, Wilson took his statist approach too far, regulating virtually every aspect of the economy with the War Industries Board during World War I and attempting to link the destiny of the United States to Europe and the rest of the world with the League of Nations, a backlash ensued, sweeping progressives out of office in the 1920s.

The progressives returned to power in the 1930s with FDR's administration. To respond to the challenges of the Great Depression, FDR experimented with different policies and approaches, ultimately favoring massive expansion of government and consolidation of powers in the executive branch. This statist perspective went largely unchallenged for decades. Bipartisan consensus for it was on public display when President Richard M. Nixon proclaimed, "We are all Keynesians now." Keynesian economics, named after the progressive economist John Maynard Keynes, was a philosophical approach that advocated government spending to stimulate the economy to promote full employment. It was only disrupted when President Reagan was elected in 1980. However, Reagan's ability to completely transform the political landscape was limited, and all presidents since, both Democrat and Republican, have embraced statist policies.

Progressives have stitched together political majorities in part because of the perception that they best advance the cause of minorities. This is false. Founding principles offer more to advance equal opportunity for women and minorities than Hegelian, statist principles. The ideals professed in the Declaration of Independence and secured in the Constitution advance *individual*, not collective rights. Conservatives share the blame for the confusion. When conservatives abandon founding principles and oppose equal opportunity and equal protection under the law, they open the space for statist progressives to be the champions of individual rights. Conservatives need to rediscover founding principles. While it is important for all constituencies, taking consistent positions promoting equal opportunity and equal protection under the law is a major issue for many in the Millennial generation. They are watching conservatives closely, and their support will be contingent on what we do.

—————

There is more at stake. In their powerfully analytical book *Habits of the Heart*, published in 1985, Robert Bellah and his coauthors offered a compelling narrative of why Americans became increasingly unhappy despite rising standards of living since the end of World War II. In moving testimonials, individuals described lacking relationships with God, family, and friends. Although blessed with material success, many Americans felt a crisis of meaning because they had no one with whom to share it. The main point of the book was that changes in American political culture in the twentieth century caused us to lose focus on the important things in life, which was a major force behind the surge in unhappiness.

The post–World War II wholesale adoption of materialism has made our politics more dysfunctional and selfish, accelerating our fiscal and moral decline. American culture, competitive since the founding, has morphed into navel gazing—who among us has the most and best of anything: cars, homes, vacations, gadgets, wealth, and the list goes on. The accumulation of worldly things for the purpose of accumulating worldly things. How can it be that a country of people blessed with so much is so unhappy? This obsession with materialism has led to an undernourishment of the soul and a crisis of meaning.

Meanwhile, political opportunists continue to promise to give us more. It never ends. This dynamic will lead to bankruptcy in more ways than one. In the past four decades, our national debt has gone from approximately $1 trillion to $20 trillion, and we have yet to enact significant legislation to balance the budget.

This was a major issue for me and why in Congress I supported the Cooper-LaTourette bipartisan budget in 2012. This budget was the Simpson-Bowles deficit reduction commission alternative offered that year. Had we enacted it, we would have balanced the budget by now and begun to pay down the debt. Unfortunately, determined partisan forces in both parties decisively defeated it. That was typical for budget matters during my six years in Congress. Republicans and Democrats kept holding out for a Napoleonic-style total victory on the political battlefield, where they would completely wipe out their opposition so that they could implement a budget 100 percent to their liking. It never happened, and we continued down the path of fiscal irresponsibility, racking up deficits and "kicking the can down the road," waiting for that ever-elusive period of one-party political dominance. Meanwhile, what's going on right now is nothing short of generational theft, putting the community and future generations at peril—and both major political parties are to blame. On the current course, we will fiscally bankrupt the nation.

While we slide into fiscal crisis, we are also experiencing a moral decline. We are searching for answers in all the wrong places. As humans, we have material needs, but we are essentially soulful beings. To revitalize our republic, we must bring that back into focus. We must recognize that we cannot solve all of our ills with abject materialism. We have lost a sense of balance. Today, with the Internet, email, social media, and cable TV, we are more connected than ever. Yet feelings of alienation abound—suicide attempts and completions are at all-time highs. It would be easy to pin all of this on the leaders of government and business, but as H. L. Mencken once told us, Americans get exactly the democracy they deserve. The leaders of government and captains of industry respond to the will of the American people. Our most profound problems are not political, they are fundamentally philosophical—what we value and how we choose to approach, organize, and live our lives. The erosion of our political culture must be addressed.

———

Abandoning founding principles has come at a high cost. For the citizen, it has meant less liberty, less upward mobility, and less happiness, and as a people we have created a crisis of confidence in self-governance. Today more than ever, Americans across the ideological spectrum feel as if the entire system is rigged for those with money, influence, and power. The ordinary hardworking taxpayer loses every time.

Our abandonment of founding principles has also eroded the separation of powers, fomenting uncertainty regarding the rules for policy dispute resolution. If we are not following the Constitution, then what are the new rules? All of this is undermining the rule of law, which has been the bedrock of our political stability and success.

Both major political parties have contributed to this development. We have lost our way as a people, and this did not occur overnight. We wandered off course discernibly decades ago when we chose to abandon balanced approaches in our constitutional arrangement and our political culture. We have put our faith in an empowered state and consolidated that power increasingly in one person. Pressure from the people to provide more and more has transformed the political process, exacerbating our fiscal crisis. This has been coupled with excessive emphasis on materialism, undermining our moral strength. We are heading down a well-traveled road. If we look closely, we will see the souls of Greek and Roman citizens warning us of what lies ahead.

Cincinnatus and Republican Virtue

If we are fortunate, we'll learn from Cincinnatus, who saved the early Roman Republic. A statesmen, citizen-soldier, and farmer, in the fifth century BC, Cincinnatus left his plow at the behest of his fellow countrymen to take command of the legions to defeat an army that threatened the Republic. In the aftermath, he could have had it all. With command of the legions, he carried the title of dictator. He could have consolidated power and enjoyed the trappings of a life befitting a Roman ruler. He did just the opposite. After achieving victory against long odds, Cincinnatus immediately resigned his post and returned to his farm. Before he was done with history, incredibly this would happen a second time, after he was again pressed into the role of dictator to lead the army to save the Republic, only to swiftly resign again afterward. His actions became legend and over the centuries served as a model of republican virtue.

Our country needs someone like Cincinnatus right now— a self-abnegating president who restores liberty and the rightful station of the legislative branch so that we can revitalize our republic. We need a president committed to founding principles, not the continued accumulation of executive powers. We need a president who campaigns for office with the pledge of returning power back to the people and the people's representatives. That has never happened before, but after the 2016 presidential campaign, anything is possible.

A Twenty-First-Century Federal Government

Here's a platform for that presidential candidate. These reforms will restore founding principles and bring balance to our constitutional arrangement and political culture. In the process, we will advance liberty, empower the people's representatives, and reform our political process, revitalizing faith in our ability to be self-governing.

1. The Regulations from the Executive In Need of Scrutiny, or REINS Act. The REINS Act ensures that any proposed new bureaucratic rule that has an estimated impact on the economy of $100 million or greater must first be approved by the people's representatives in Congress. This bill passed in the House of Representatives in each of the 112th, 113th, and 114th Congresses. Unfortunately, it was never considered in the Senate. The *Wall Street Journal* accurately assessed that this bill would provide the most sweeping reform of the regulatory process since the end of World War II, and in the process help unleash significant economic growth. Although the REINS Act would make the job of a representative harder, I voted for this bill every time, because this reform is needed to check an overreaching executive branch. At a time when people are frustrated by the lack of transparency and accountability in our bureaucracy, the bill would ensure that the people get a voice in this process through their elected representative. It would also inject more common sense into the regulatory process, which has hampered economic growth in recent decades. This simple reform would increase confidence and competence in our federal government and facilitate more prosperity for the American people.

2. Budget reform. As part of the effort to empower the legislative branch, we must enact comprehensive budget reform. The 1974 Budget Act, enacted in an era of high inflation, has been a failure and must be overhauled. At the time, legislators wanted to avoid taking hard votes that significantly increased government spending to keep up with runaway inflation, so they introduced the concept of "baseline budgeting" that automatically increased government accounts annually, even if they didn't need it. The 1974 Budget Act has contributed to massive deficits and essentially passed along critical decisions on the proper levels of spending from the legislative to the executive branch. To change that we must enact *"zero-based budgeting,"* in which expenditures for every account must be justified each and every year. Zero-based budgeting will reclaim legislative powers for the Congress and ensure that we properly fund necessary federal requirements and reduce expenditures in areas where programs are failing or no longer needed.

Second, we should *change the filibuster rule in the Senate that requires sixty votes to enact budget and appropriations bills.* It was very frustrating over the years to pass many appropriations bills in the House, only to see them filibustered in the Senate, which was unable to muster sixty votes for cloture. The minority party in Congress should not be able to stop government from doing its most essential work. If the president vetoes a spending bill, then further accommodation is required to enact the bill, but in many cases a bipartisan appropriations bill in the House of Representatives was not even considered in the Senate, due to the decision of the minority leader. Keeping the filibuster for policy-related bills may make sense, but for spending bills this must change. Our country's federal departments must be funded. This gridlock has created enormous frustration among the American people, requiring multiple continuing resolutions (CRs) to keep the government running. In a related way, both houses should adopt a rule that limits appropriations for the respective federal departments to individual bills—*no more so-called omnibus spending bills* that lead to pork-barrel inclusion and, subsequently, significant disillusionment among the electorate.

We should make three final reforms when changing budget procedures. We should *move to biannual budgeting, change the*

*beginning of the fiscal year from October 1 to January 1, and adopt
"no budget, no pay" for legislators.* Establishing a budget for each
Congress (a two-year period) would enable Congress to focus on
the annual appropriations bills (the real "power of the purse")
and the critical function of oversight of federal departments.
Also, since 1974 we have never had a year where all appropriations bills were completed by October 1—that's simply an unrealistic timeline. We should move the beginning of the fiscal year
to correspond with the calendar year. The devastating impacts
on national security readiness alone, which is adversely affected
by CRs, should provide enough justification to get that done.
Finally, members of Congress should not be paid if they cannot
fulfill their basic function of funding government.

Enacting budget reform will restore the legislative branch's
Article I powers under the Constitution and help government
run more efficiently and effectively. It will also go a long way in
addressing many of the frustrations of the American people with
their political process, helping restore faith in our republic.

3. The Separation of Powers Restoration Act. This bill passed
in the House of Representatives in the 114th Congress but was never
considered in the Senate. The Separation of Powers Restoration Act
provides clarity regarding the responsibilities of the Congress as initially outlined by the Founders in the Constitution by reasserting
the legislative branch's Article I powers. This bill will promote liberty and empower and hold accountable the people's representatives.
It will help reverse the trend of consolidation and centralization of
power in the executive branch, which has adversely impacted our
constitutional arrangement and political culture for more than seventy years. An emotionally and politically secure president, inspired
to restore republican values and founding principles, will sign that
legislation for the good of the country.

4. The War Powers Reform Act. Finally, regarding the legislative-executive branch relationship, we must address the war powers authority. To avoid the abuses of King George, the Founders clearly intended for these powers to reside with the people's representatives in Congress. This is no longer the case. We have consolidated war powers authority in the executive branch, and presidents from both political parties have employed force without the express permission of Congress. We must enact the War Powers Reform Act. I authored this bill in each of the 112th, 113th, and 114th Congresses, and although it garnered significant bipartisan support, it never received a vote. This bill would ensure that the American people get a voice, through their elected representatives, before the nation makes the solemn decision on the use of force. I believe it would not only help address the legislative-executive branch power relationship, but it would also enhance the "peace through strength" approach to national security. By forcing Congress to take a recorded vote *before* we send our troops off to war, we would likely see more robust debate and fewer cases in which we use military force.

5. Supreme Court independence. To fully revitalize the separation of powers, we need to restore the independence of the judiciary branch. The courts have been increasingly politicized. The Founders intended for the courts to be an independent branch, checking the powers of Congress and the president, ensuring the preservation of liberty. Today, some, including myself, wonder if we have come full circle to pre-Revolution days when the Court was just an extension of the executive. When presidential candidates require litmus tests for Supreme Court consideration, how is that any different from the days when King George picked judges based on his perception of their willingness to carry out his justice? Although new legislation may not be appropriate, we could benefit from new norms. Presidential leadership could be decisive. Presidential candidates should pledge to select justices based on only two criteria—integrity and a record of interpreting laws in accordance with the Constitution. My former colleagues Justin Amash, Raúl Labrador, and Trey Gowdy are three examples of individuals who meet that description.

6. Political reform. Finally, to help revitalize the republic and restore faith in our ability to be self-governing, we need several political reforms, changes to the way we send representatives to Congress. The whole point of our founding was to put the citizen at the center of government. Today most Americans no longer believe that is the case. The influence of money has drowned out the voice of ordinary citizens, giving disproportionate power to the wealthiest Americans. It is past time that we rectify that. We need a simple *campaign finance amendment* to the Constitution that states something to the effect of, "In view of the spirit one person, one vote, the Congress shall have the power to regulate federal election campaigns." Although critics would say that the Congress already has that power, in the past, every time a significant reform has been enacted, the Supreme Court has eviscerated it, asserting infringement of "free speech." As someone who has gone through this, I assure all, there is nothing "free" about that speech. It's very expensive! A constitutional amendment would send a signal to the courts that the people support such reforms.

Once a new constitutional amendment is in place, Congress should enact a series of reforms that include capping congressional spending limits, full disclosure of all donations, and the prohibition of *all* outside spending. All political action committees (business, labor, outside groups, and Super PACs) should be banned from making political donations. Political donations should be limited to U.S. citizens eligible to vote, and the amount that they can contribute should be limited to reasonable amounts similar to what is on the books today. In Congress, I led on this issue. In my 2014 reelection race, I proposed to my opponent that we adopt these standards. Unfortunately, he rejected the offer, which was a shame. Had he accepted, we could have set a positive example for the nation and helped build momentum for campaign finance reform of the right kind. To be clear, I oppose public financing of campaigns. That is not a good use of taxpayer dollars. With $20 trillion in debt and more investments needed in national security and infrastructure, the last thing we need to do is give taxpayer dollars to politicians, especially when most expenditures go toward negative campaign advertising. We can achieve desired objectives with the aforementioned framework.

Next, we must address the political culture and mind-set in Congress. Service in Congress should be a calling to serve a self-governing people—not a career. As we have now for the presidency, we need to enact *term limits for members of Congress.* There are several different specific term-limit policy proposals out there, and I've supported a few of them over the years, ultimately self-imposing my own at six years. Probably the best proposal is to cap service in each house at twelve years. That is ample time to make a significant difference and ensure that the process remains member- and not staff-driven, while eliminating the downsides of a permanent political class in Washington. In an ideal world, we would not need term limits, as the ballot box would serve that function. But we don't live in an ideal world. We live in the real world where the power of incumbency stacks the deck against the power of the people. It's past time to change that. To get the votes necessary to enact this legislation, we may need to grandfather its implementation. Such a pragmatic approach would ultimately achieve the desired policy effect and, from a political perspective, increase the changes of its enactment.

We also need an *independent redistricting amendment* to the Constitution. We have the illusion that we pick our representatives, when too often representatives pick their voters every ten years through the redistricting process. The media focuses on partisan gridlock in Congress, but it completely misses the bipartisan collusion that occurs every ten years after the census is completed and the states go about the reapportionment and redistricting process. The real loser in that dynamic is the people, who see their influence significantly decreased through gerrymandering that serves only powerful politicians—incumbents. That must change. To remain consistent with the Constitution and our approach of federalism, this may need to be a broad national mandate with implementation left to the states.

Last, we must stop the revolving door between Congress and the lobbying industry. We need *tougher standards on lobbying for former members.* The temptation is real that members could be influenced by lobbyists if they believe their actions may get them hired as lobbyists after congressional service. We should take that off the table. Currently there is a one-year ban in effect. The Trump administration has proposed a five-year ban for those who serve in the executive branch, and Congress should codify that while applying the same standard for themselves.

Candidate Trump pledged to "drain the swamp." Now that he is in office, we should hold him to that pledge. Opinion polls confirm that the American people believe our political system is corrupt and rigged against them. By enacting political reform, we can restore trust with the American people. The American people are ready to restore founding principles. What's needed is strong, selfless leadership to take us there. It won't happen without presidential leadership, especially since part of what must be done includes sending some executive powers back to the legislative branch. We can take inspiration from our first president, George Washington, who viewed Cincinnatus as a role model of republican virtue.

As the Revolutionary War was coming to a close, some military officers were so upset by Congress's inability to pay Continental Army soldiers that they concocted a plan while encamped at Newburgh, New York, to have General Washington coerce them to pay at the threat of a coup. General Washington rejected their urgings, quashing the "Newburgh Conspiracy." He then rode to Washington, D.C., and turned in his commission to the Continental Congress. He wanted to make it clear that he had not spent all those years fighting for liberty to give it away to military dictatorship. Like Cincinnatus, Washington refused absolute power and saved the republic. When he voluntarily stepped down to return to the farm after his second term as president, he saved the republic a second time like his Roman role model.

That's the kind of selfless leader we need now to restore founding principles and revitalize the American dream. This is an extraordinary nation—exceptional since its birth. Against long odds, our Founders established a self-governing republic conceived in liberty. What they did was truly miraculous, and it changed the course of world history. We can do it again.

CHAPTER 3

Promote a Flourishing Life

The Urgency of Now

There is widespread unhappiness across the land. From working-class Americans to billionaires and across the ideological spectrum and political divide there is deep disappointment in the state of politics and general direction of our country. That angst was palpable and visible for all to see at rallies for both Donald Trump and Bernie Sanders during the last presidential campaign. The entire American way of life is being questioned and there is widespread belief that our system is rigged.

People demand change and are willing to go to places they've never been before to get it. In the words of one of my constituents in the summer of 2015, "Donald Trump may not be the answer, but he is the middle finger." The election brought a change in leadership and now is the time to deliver. In this chapter I discuss how to get the economy going so that all citizens have a shot at the American dream.

Eudaimonia

Let's start by putting the American dream in proper context and then defining it. For that, we look to the founding era. "Life, liberty, and the pursuit of happiness"—those were the words Thomas Jefferson settled on for describing our God-given natural rights in the Declaration of Independence. It was a bold move. Up until that point in history, philosophers embraced John Locke's definition of natural rights consisting of "life, liberty, and property."

Of course, the Founders were not opposed to property rights. They assumed that property ownership was inherent in the rights of free men. Rather, this was an audacious statement concerning *human potential* and government's role protecting and promoting it. For the ancient Greeks, the person constantly seeking self-improvement, committing themselves to the pursuit of intellectual, spiritual, moral, and physical excellence, was living a eudaimonic life. Over the centuries, "eudaimonia" has been translated in different ways. In the late eighteenth century, it was translated into English as "happiness," which is why Jefferson put "pursuit of happiness" in the Declaration of Independence. In some ways that was a shame, because today most Americans read that word in context as some vague statement about physical or emotional pleasures. Jefferson intended for it to mean that humans have the right to pursue excellence and rise to their God-given potential. Instead of "and the pursuit of happiness," it should have read "and a flourishing life."

Probably the best way to understand eudaimonia in the modern context is found in the writings of psychologist Abraham Maslow. In his groundbreaking paper published in *Psychological Review* in 1943, Maslow argued that humans have a hierarchy of needs. These proceed from basic physical requirements such as oxygen, water, sustenance, shelter, and security, to social needs of love, belongingness, and esteem, to the ultimate human condition of "self-actualization." They are hierarchal because if you don't have food, water, or security, then achieving self-actualization is moot. Maslow gave us a practical approach to understanding human behavior and a thoughtful explanation for what makes us satisfied. The Founders' bold move was declaring before the world that God intended for us to strive for self-actualization. This was not a destination or a final achievement but rather a *state of flourishing*—constantly pursuing intellectual, spiritual, moral, and physical *excellence*.

Pursuing a flourishing life *is* the American dream. We desire higher education or career and technical certification to prepare to excel in the professional world. The pursuit of excellence motivates us to run marathons, climb mountains, go to Army Ranger school, or volunteer at Habitat for Humanity. We push ourselves to be better, achieve hard things—we are constantly in pursuit of a better self. Our political culture at the founding was blended, and as we individually sought to reach our God-given potential, we balanced that priority with our obligations to family, friends, and the community. Thus the American dream also included working hard so that our children could have a better life than us, and giving back to our community to make it better and stronger.

The Founders deeply believed that these desires and actions, "the pursuit of happiness," were part of what it meant to be human. Prior to the Revolution, people across the earth were trapped in a life with no prospect of upward mobility and little chance for self-improvement. If you were born a serf, you died a serf. To the Founders, such an existence was not a life at all. They declared before the world that humans have the God-given right to a flourishing life. This was our dream—*the American dream*.

The Dignity of Work

The pursuit of professional excellence occurs within the economy. In some ways an economy is like a machine, with many different parts that must all work together in an integrated fashion. The economy of the 19th Congressional District in New York is very diverse, with farms, manufacturing facilities, construction companies and unions, schools, health care facilities, government agencies, and small businesses that support all these activities.

———

The foundation of our economy is built upon hard work. No one understood that better than Dr. Martin Luther King Jr., who was a tireless advocate for equal opportunity and social justice and an inspiration for all Americans. It was an incredibly powerful feeling the day I learned in history class that Dr. King had gone to Memphis to advocate for sanitation workers on strike. During that time, my dad was out of work on strike too. The video showed Dr. King speaking at a church, proclaiming emphatically that *every human had dignity, and every job had value.* All of a sudden I felt better about Dad. King was praising manual laborers like my dad and fighting on their behalf. It gave me hope that maybe Dad would get back to work soon. When he was working, he was happier and carried himself with pride. When he wasn't working, nothing seemed to please him. Work gave Dad dignity.

We need to rediscover Dr. King's message. Every job has value. We need manual laborers, technicians, entrepreneurs, farmers, nurses, doctors, teachers, and many other professions and occupations. Unfortunately, society today too often denigrates manual labor, and that's part of the reason we are struggling. I started doing janitorial work, then served as a clerk and infantry private, before ultimately rising to be an Army colonel and U.S. congressman. They were all important jobs, and I'm certainly better off because of those early manual labor experiences. Let us remember Dr. King's summoning words:

> If a man is called to be a street sweeper, he should sweep streets even as a Michelangelo painted, or Beethoven composed music or Shakespeare wrote poetry. He should sweep streets so well that all the hosts of heaven and earth will pause to say, "Here lived a great street sweeper who did his job well." No work is insignificant. All labor that uplifts humanity has dignity and importance and should be undertaken with painstaking excellence.

Dairy Boot Camp

In March 2010, I retired from the Army to run for Congress. Although I grew up in rural Columbia County in upstate New York, and there isn't a single dairy product I don't love, I knew next to nothing about dairy farming. There are over five hundred major dairy operations in the district, and if I aspired to represent them, I needed to know their challenges—really know them. I asked one of my neighbors in Kinderhook, Eric Ooms, a second-generation American and hardworking dairy farmer, if I could attend "dairy boot camp" on his farm.

After first laughing at me, then realizing I was serious, he agreed. I reported for duty one cold February morning at 3:30 a.m. The day began with preparation to milk cows. By 4:00 a.m., we were moving cows into the milking stalls. With over 350 cows, this task took nearly two hours. With electric milking machines, the key is to get the cow in the right place and properly attach the line to the teat. Then you must keep the flow going until milking is finished, before getting the cows back to their grazing areas or stalls. After milking, the next task was to feed the cows. Eric's brother Tim was in charge of that. We were blending grains and protein sources to maximize nutritional value. It was important to get the mix just right, as the quality of the milk and the overall health of the animal (including long-term milking viability and ability to reproduce) depend on proper nutrition. Thereafter, I was put on cow stall cleanup duty. There's really no way to euphemistically explain this one. It's just Mother Nature taking its course as cows do what cows must do, and cleaning up after them is dirty work that plainly must be accomplished. In some ways, this was perfect preparation for Congress!

Eric Ooms (left) and Tim Ooms (center) explaining feeding operations during "dairy boot camp." *Credit: Lance Wheeler*

By then it was about 9:30, and we took a break for a nice breakfast with the entire Ooms family. Eric's wife prepared awesome country fare—eggs, bacon, pancakes and syrup, and of course, fresh raw milk. Eric and Tim's dad, Adrian, was there. Adrian immigrated from the Netherlands in 1950. The Ooms family traces their dairy farming roots back to the sixteenth century in the old country. When they arrived in America, Adrian and his brother had no money and spoke little English, but they had an unparalleled work ethic and a hunger for success. They have lived the American dream. Today Adrian is retired but holds an emeritus status in the family, which keeps Eric and Tim on task. The family business thrives, even in difficult circumstances for dairy farmers.

The discussion at breakfast was lively. Adrian is a staunch conservative and he had a lot to say about government overreach, particularly as it relates to regulation. Concentrated animal feeding operation (CAFO) regulations micromanage the farming process, rather than just evaluating them on the quality of their product and stewardship of their farm. Farmers chafe over this because strong environmental practices are already in their best interests. If they pollute their land, they ultimately put themselves out of business. Farmers prefer instead the incentivized approach of conservation programs that provide a federal share of cost when they invest in fencing to stop cows from answering nature's call in the nearby streams. As we enjoyed breakfast, Adrian gave me an earful on what it would mean to the Ooms farm if the Obama administration's proposed rule on spilled milk went into effect.

I also had the opportunity to learn about business operations. The Ooms family participates in a co-op that picks up their milk and brings it to a processor with Agri-Mark of Cabot Creamery. Being part of the co-op provides them with consistency, a predictable schedule for the sale of their product. How much dairy farmers actually get in their "milk check," however, is a source of enormous frustration. For about a century, the amount in the milk check has been highly dependent on the price of cheese in the futures market in Chicago. Farmers express dissatisfaction with this process, since it is based on a narrow measurement of supply and demand and doesn't account for regional dynamics. The major fluctuations in the milk check play havoc on a farmer's business plan. Milk checks go up and down, but costs stay fairly stable, and high. Here's what it means for dairy farmers. A gallon of milk today may cost a consumer $3.75, but the dairy farmer only gets $1.35 in that transaction. Although someone is making a lot of money in the process, it's not the dairy farmer.

In the farm bill of 2013, we tried to leaven out the wild oscillations in payments for dairy farmers by instituting a voluntary margin insurance program that takes into account the costs of inputs and the farmer's milk check. It was well-intentioned, but it has not worked. Farmers are losing money and still paying for an insurance that is doing them little, if any, good. What is needed is a comprehensive examination of the entire enterprise—we need full transparency in price discovery and farmer payment. Given what consumers are paying for milk, dairy farmers should be able to make a decent living, but presently they are struggling.

Farmers are counting on us to make smart trade agreements that are in the best interests of our nation. Part of the problem with the proposed Trans-Pacific Partnership (TPP) is that one of the twelve nations in the tentative pact, New Zealand, has a command economy (essentially a socialistic government) and a burgeoning dairy sector that receives special help from its government, making our dairy industry uncompetitive with them. Under the current draft, New Zealand gets a decided advantage over us because there are no prohibitions against subsidizing dairy products at the point of export. This enables the New Zealand government to essentially undercut every American bid in the marketplace. Thus TPP has the potential to do the kind of harm to our agricultural sector that the North American Free Trade Agreement (NAFTA) did to our manufacturing sector.

At one point several years ago, exports represented 18 percent of the U.S. dairy market. Today that figure is around 13 percent. In part this is due to the embargo we put on Russia after their invasion of Crimea in 2014. The increasing strength of the U.S. dollar over the past couple of years has also caused a decline in exports. The bottom line is that we need smart trade agreements that put our farmers on a level playing field with our competitors to help us regain global market share.

The Oomses also worry about labor costs. Given the declining propensity of Americans to work on farms and the impasse regarding immigration reform, all farmers, including dairy farmers, list access to reliable labor as among their top concerns. This must be addressed or the American family farm will disappear. An independent nation must be able to produce its own food, and losing family farms has national security impact.

Welfare reform could help by incentivizing more Americans to work on farms. We also need to address the agricultural guest-worker program. The federal government H-2A program, which provides temporary visas for foreigners to work on our farms, is broken. In an attempt to fix this challenging problem, I introduced a bill to reform the H-2A program to ensure that farmers had access to reliable and legal workers. My bill, which attracted bipartisan support, moved jurisdiction of the program from the Department of Labor to the Department of Agriculture, whose employees are much more sympathetic to the plight of farmers. The bill also required the entire application process to be done online, because too many times our farmers submitted requests and were never given feedback. At the last minute, some were told, "Your application is incomplete." That's not helpful at all. With the online system, if an application is incomplete, the applicant gets an error message and has to rectify the problem on the spot before the request is officially accepted. The online process also enables farmers to track progress until their requested workers arrive on the farm. When fixed, the H-2A program will allow farmers to gain access to motivated, reliable workers who come to the United States for a designated period of time, work hard and abide by our laws, and then return home to their country.

After breakfast at dairy boot camp, we went back to work doing chores on the farm, including inspecting for cow manure the cesspool that was constructed with the help of federal funds available for conservation. Then, in the early afternoon, it was time for the second iteration of milking, feeding, and cleaning. All that lasted until dinner. It was a long day, starting with a wake-up at 3:00 a.m. and ending around 6:00 p.m. I was tired but it felt good, reminding me of my infantry days. What struck me as I was driving home was that Eric and Tim were going to do it all over again starting at 3:00 in the morning the next day. They do that each day, every day. They do it in the driving rain, in the snow, in subzero temperatures, and on days when the thermostat reaches 100 degrees or more. Renowned economist John Kenneth Galbraith once said, "If you have ever worked on a farm, nothing else ever seems like work." After dairy boot camp, I can relate. Farming is a calling. Farmers love what they do—they know they grow and raise the food that feeds America, and they are very proud of that.

The Breadbasket of the American Revolution

The Hudson Valley region of New York was once the breadbasket of the American Revolution, producing much of the food that fed our Continental Army soldiers. Over the years, like in so many places around our country, the number of farms and farmers there steadily declined. That trend came to an abrupt halt in 2010. According to the census taken that year, for the first time in over fifty years we are now growing the number of family farms.

This is very good news. By producing and consuming locally, we support better nutrition habits that will enable us to live longer and healthier lives, while reducing health care costs. Supporting local farmers also helps grow our local economy and provide jobs and additional revenues for local governments, which helps keep property taxes lower, a major concern for New York State and across the country.

To keep this positive trend going, we need to reform our federal policies. In some areas we need more support, and in others (like regulation) we need government to pull back. As I prepared to advocate for our farmers in the farm bill reauthorization process of 2013, I benefited enormously from my advisory panel. Led by Michael Bittel and comprising dozens of farmers and agricultural experts from throughout upstate New York, they educated us on all facets of federal policy. On fruits and vegetables, a young couple from Columbia County played a tremendous role in crafting legislation that later became law. Lindsey and Ben Shute own Hearty Roots Farm in Clermont. They represent a new brand of agricultural entrepreneurs, many specializing in organic operations. In addition to being hardworking, these newer "greenhorn" farmers are politically organized and vocal. Lindsey is a leader in the National Young Farmers Coalition. They are effective advocates for promoting federal and state policies to help beginning farmers. I met with Lindsey and she provided extensive education on their issues. After a series of meetings, we were ready to draft legislation.

Working with Representative Tim Walz, the same member with whom I sponsored the Posture Act, I introduced the Beginning Farmer and Rancher Opportunity Act. This bill literally and figuratively helps beginning farmers get their roots in the ground during that initial decade of operation, when they are most vulnerable. To understand the essence of this bill, the key word is "access." The bill helps provide access to land (beginning farmers' number one issue) by amending tax policy to make it advantageous for retiring farmers to bring on apprentices and transition that land to the aspiring beginning farmer. The bill also provides access to credit, with a newly devised microloan program for beginning farmers. This enables young farmers to purchase seed, machinery, and other requirements to get under way. The bill also helps beginning farmers with access to discounts on insurance and special provisions in the conservation programs to ensure that their payments are up front to ease cash flow challenges. Finally, the bill also provides access to training, not just approaches to farming, but also business practices. For beginning farmers, the margin for error is slim; one mistake on bookkeeping or inventory could potentially lead to bankruptcy.

Hawthorne Valley Farm in Philmont hosts beginning farmer training. Its owner, Martin Ping, is an awesome teacher who spends lots of time mentoring aspiring young farmers. I spent half a day with him to learn his approaches and to appreciate the challenges. In addition to the farm, Ping runs a private secondary school, which beyond the standard curriculum teaches agricultural studies and unique courses like one inspired by the ancient Greeks on "balance." The pedagogy is based heavily on hands-on practice and applied methods. The renaissance in farming in the Hudson Valley is in large part because of this mentorship program that falls under the auspice of the federal Beginning Farmer Program.

Representative Walz and I were successful getting our Beginning Farmer and Rancher Opportunity Act included in the farm bill enacted in 2013. After the president signed that bill into law, I returned to Hawthorne Valley Farm to do a press conference explaining the bill to my constituents. Ultimately, the bill's passage was not only a big win for our beginning farmers, but it also helped restore faith in our ability to be self-governing. Lindsey Shute is not a registered lobbyist—she is a proud farmer. Yet she also helped craft a bill that became law in our country. We are a government "of the people, by the people, for the people," and this experience reinforced that.

———

Agriculture is the number one driver of our rural economies, and strengthening family farms must be a priority. Policy initiatives that will help include reforming dairy policies to properly pay farmers for their milk, enacting regulatory relief and reform, reforming welfare and agricultural worker programs so that farmers have access to a reliable workforce, negotiating good trade deals that put our farmers on a level playing field, and fully supporting policies like the Beginning Farmer and Rancher Opportunity Act. All of these initiatives are needed to help strengthen the rural economy, which has struggled for decades.

We are poised for an agricultural comeback. Even as we strive for excellence in the twenty-first-century information age economy, we still need to feed our people, and for that our family farms must flourish. Our farmers don't expect to get rich, but they do expect to be fairly compensated and make a living in exchange for their hard work that feeds this country. Our farmers and their workers need our support. We must enact reforms to ensure that they sustain a flourishing life. As the 2016 election proved, rural America is up for grabs and can definitely make a difference to the outcome of a national election. As the Congress looks forward to the 2018 farm bill reauthorization process, political leaders would be wise to take note.

Big Company in a Little Town

The Amphenol Corporation has been in Sidney, New York, for over seventy-five years, and at close to one thousand employees plays an absolutely essential role in this small, rural town of roughly five thousand people in central New York. Amphenol grew significantly during World War II, providing electrical connectors, a critical component that joins parts to create an electrical circuit, bringing to life our aircraft, weapons systems, and radios. Over the years the corporation has changed names and gone through acquisitions and mergers, but through it all has been a constant presence in the area.

My visits to Amphenol have been productive and enjoyable. Loyalty is very strong—many workers have been there for more than thirty years, and some are legacies, with their parents alumni as well. Having spent twenty-nine years in the military, I know their connectors played a key role in ensuring that we succeeded during the Persian Gulf War, and helped us defeat Al Qaeda in Iraq after 9/11. These are proud workers, and for good reason. They produce a high-quality product that our nation needs.

My first visit to Amphenol occurred during my initial campaign for Congress in the fall of 2010. As the son of a union man and a former enlisted soldier, I'm always assessing how well businesses treat their employees. At Amphenol, the first good sign on that score was that management wanted union leadership present at our meeting and to accompany us on the tour of the factory floor. That indicated a strong commitment to transparency and a sense of confidence in their management-employee relations. The meeting, which lasted about forty-five minutes, was focused and professionally relaxed. During the factory tour, workers looked me in the eye and gave me direct answers, a good sign that they felt valued and that their leaders expected them to tell it like it is.

I learned that some of the workers had concerns about whether Amphenol would stay in Sidney for the long haul. When I finished the tour, I engaged with the local executive, Rick Aiken, about what I had heard from the workers. Rick was very candid. Amphenol leadership was disappointed with local federal and state officials for not being more empathetic and supportive about their plight following a major flood in 2006, while I was still in the Army. He communicated that if another flood hit, they were "out of here."

It came the following year in August, and when it did, it was devastating. Back-to-back devastating natural disasters Irene and Lee crushed my congressional district and took several lives. Helping lead the recovery effort in the Congress immediately became our top priority for the next year. We helped deliver hundreds of millions of dollars of storm aid to our region. We had small rural communities, like Prattsville and Schoharie, where a majority of the inhabitants were homeless after the floods from the hurricane. The force of the water flowing down main street in Prattsville exceeded that of Niagara Falls. Sidney was ground zero for Tropical Storm

Lee, which hit about a week after Irene. It caused the Susquehanna River to come off the rails, flooding downtown Sidney, leaving many residents homeless, and inflicting major damage on the Amphenol site for the second time in only five years.

The first call came from Sidney mayor Andy Matviak. The situation was dire. "We need you here now." When my district director, Steve Bulger, and I arrived the next day, the situation was beyond belief—destruction everywhere. I felt like I was in a war zone again. The Amphenol leadership had quickly ordered evacuation to a temporary site, an old hospital on higher ground, to ensure that they could continue to meet their orders, which were essential to the Joint Strike Fighter and other critical national assets. Everyone in the company was completely involved in the manual labor supporting that evacuation. Since many of the employees lived in the village, they also had the added hardship of being homeless and concerned for their families.

When Andy and I met with Rick Aiken, and his boss Gary Anderson from Amphenol corporate headquarters, the initial feeling was awkward and somewhat hostile. Anderson in particular was loaded for bear. He initially refused to meet with me; he wanted no part of "worthless politicians." Both Matviak and Aiken pleaded with him, "Give him a chance. He's a former soldier." Anderson relented, but his skepticism was on display as we greeted each other. He didn't try to hide his contempt and did nothing to assuage my concern for the future of Amphenol's presence in Sidney. "I welcome any help you can provide, but we're likely out of here soon anyway," Anderson stated. Still upset by the lack of help back in 2006, he was apoplectic. "This is what happens when no one in the federal government listens to those who know what they are talking about!"

He toured me around both the destroyed facility and the

temporary relocation site. Bulger and I took copious notes and listened to all testimonials and requests. At the end of our time together, Anderson said, "If we can't get our Internet up tonight, we will lose our business. Do you understand?"

I confirmed I did. As Bulger and I departed, I knew we needed to move mountains for Amphenol, the village of Sidney, and so many other communities across our congressional district. We went right to work. The first thing we did was get that Internet connection up. Fortunately, we had built relationships with most companies in and around our district. I called Time Warner Cable for help. Their government relations officer, Rory Whelan, told us he would work on it first thing Monday morning (it was a Sunday). I expressed my appreciation but pleaded, "It can't wait until then. We need it back up today." His team got that mission done.

Sometimes it's the little things in life that make all the difference. I'm told by Rick Aiken and Mayor Matviak that this effective response, getting the Internet going on the same day requested, impressed Anderson and helped build trust to work with him to hopefully keep Amphenol in Sidney.

I worked closely with my friend and colleague Representative Peter Welch, Democrat of Vermont, to get flood recovery money for our districts and the region. Our efforts were successful. Over a series of appropriations bills, first in a continuing resolution in September and later in an appropriations bill in December, we secured over a billion dollars for areas in the Northeast impacted by these natural disasters.

To keep Amphenol in Sidney after the flood took much more work, however. Fortunately, Senator Chuck Schumer provided significant assistance, and Governor Andrew Cuomo also pitched in. Eventually, we were able to secure a $20 million package to help relocate Amphenol about a mile or so from the temporary site (about half a mile from their original site) to much higher ground, out of the flood zone. After intense and delicate negotiations, Amphenol agreed to accept the federal help and stay in Sidney. Today, their new site is state-of-the-art, and Amphenol's product, especially their connector, is second to none.

Beyond flood protection, Amphenol requested help with workforce development. As proud as they are of their high-performing, professional workforce, the average age of a worker is about fifty-eight years old. They were concerned about inspiring a new generation of skilled central New Yorkers to work at the plant. Company leadership wanted help preparing workers with technical skills—operating machines, welding, quality assurance, and the like. To address this concern, our office partnered with State Senator James Seward, Mayor Matviak, local chamber of commerce leader John Redente, and others to collaborate with a nearby college and the local Boards of Cooperative Educational Services (BOCES) to help train students for duty at Amphenol.

Gaining access to trained workers is a common concern among employers across our district and, as I have learned from talking with my colleagues, across the nation. Prior to 2010 our education system was not optimized to help prepare young folks for these challenges working with manufacturing companies. In the Congress, we enacted legislation to help. The Skills Act of 2014 provided federal resources and better policy to facilitate a closer relationship between business, labor, colleges, and BOCES to produce graduates prepared for the challenges of manufacturing and engineering. This emphasis on career technical work will pay off for our nation in the future. That was part of the agenda when I met with the leadership of the nearby BOCES programs. They were excited to brief me on their new Techtronics program, which will be very helpful for Amphenol and other companies across the region.

In the Joint Strike Fighter simulator. Amphenol, in Sidney, New York, provides the connectors for this aircraft. *Credit: Julie Lewis,* Daily Star

Working closely with Amphenol and other government officials, we ensured that they stayed in central New York. They now appear poised to flourish for years to come. That is good news for the roughly one thousand employees in my district who make a strong wage with good benefits. In the process, we keep our military strong, critical to the success of peace through strength. Talking with Amphenol workers, it is clear that they are proud of what they do and appreciate the company's commitment to them and their families. Keeping companies like Amphenol strong, now and in the future, is in everyone's best interest and helps facilitate a flourishing life in central New York.

Ioxus—Moving Jobs Back from Japan to Central New York

Ioxus is a small high-tech company that manufactures ultracapacitors. An ultracapacitor is like an energy drink for an engine, helping it operate with more efficiency and power. Ultracapacitors can be installed in such items as wind turbines, buses, and even Xerox machines.

Ioxus is located in Oneonta, New York, whose city and town comprise a little over fourteen thousand people and lie within the 19th Congressional District of New York. A fairly new company, Ioxus is just under a decade old. Their big break came when in 2012 they acquired the Power Systems Company, which had been located in Japan, with about a hundred employees manufacturing ultracapacitors for sale globally. After Ioxus acquired Power Systems, they immediately moved thirty jobs back from Japan to Oneonta. They were able to do this and make it work for their business plan by utilizing technology (specialized machines that helped improve the manufacturing process) and a better-trained and better-motivated workforce in central New York.

I visited Ioxus in 2013 and came away very impressed and optimistic about the prospects of getting more jobs back from Asia. CEO Mark McGough has his team very focused. That's necessary, because international competitors have an advantage due to our bad trade policies. Presently, U.S.-manufactured ultracapacitors sold overseas are taxed (with tariffs and value-added taxes) at a higher rate than foreign-manufactured ultracapacitors sold domestically. Unfair trade policies are hurting companies like Ioxus, which is why "fair trade" agreements are needed to ensure that our manufacturers are on a level playing field.

Despite being saddled with unfair trade practices, Ioxus is highly competitive and impressive. As I toured the factory floor and talked with workers, I learned that most had either BOCES high school education or a two-year associate's degree in career and technical skills. These workers were focused on doing their jobs to the best of their abilities. They were proud of their work and saw paths for upward mobility within the company. Pay and benefits were competitive. The chief operating officer, Philip Meek, an Army veteran, shared his experiences in uniform and how they helped him succeed in college and later take on leadership responsibilities in business. Phil brings a veteran's mission focus and service orientation to Ioxus, and that has helped his team thrive.

The workforce in Oneonta has grown to over seventy-five employees. Overall, sales are doing fine but could be improved with better U.S. trade policies. Presently, cheap imports from China and South Korea are getting a sizable portion of the U.S. domestic market. Still, Ioxus sales to companies in the United Kingdom, France, Spain, Germany, Japan, and even China are keeping this fledging, innovative company in positive territory. They are optimistic about the future.

I highlight Ioxus because they represent our country's vast potential to get jobs back from Asia. Sometimes we make our competitors out to be ten-foot-tall giants we can't defeat. In the 1980s, when I was young, the conventional wisdom was that Japan was going to bury us economically. That never happened. Similarly, today some believe that China will dominate us and relegate the United States and the rest of the world to second-rate powers. Yet China has serious labor problems and significant environmental issues, and it has built major new cities with few people in them, a development that is sure to depress the country's future commercial real estate market. For all of our challenges—and we have them, to be sure—the United States is still the best economic bet in the world. Just take a look at the market. Money doesn't lie. Investors around the globe still put their money here, because they see the potential of the American entrepreneur and the productivity of the American worker. We have the best-trained and best-motivated workforce in the world, and with our ingenuity and

This headline says it all. Hopefully the beginning of a positive trend of many jobs moving back to the United States from Asia. *Credit: Jim Kevlin,* Hometown Oneonta

desire to constantly improve, that nexus of innovation and worker excellence will dominate world markets in this century. The energy revolution in our country is already helping. By driving down overhead costs, our companies are becoming more competitive. Ioxus is a prime example of these positive developments, and they are an integral part of the future vision for Oneonta and Otsego County, a part of central New York on the march.

Ioxus employees live in small communities in the surrounding area that in many ways are typical of rural America. To help put the economy in broader context, I'll briefly sketch where the jobs and businesses are in Otsego County. The county presently has a population of roughly sixty-two thousand, and if it can get help from federal and state pro-growth policies, it is poised to see marked economic growth and quality-of-life improvements in the coming years.

I'll start in Cooperstown, approximately a thirty-minute drive from Oneonta, where the Baseball Hall of Fame is located. The hall draws over three hundred thousand visitors a year, which brings in significant revenues from tourist activities and provides a strong emotional attachment to the area for those who visit. The village is beautiful, bustling, and fun (batting cages for all ages, milkshakes, shops with old baseball cards—you really can't go wrong). The region beyond Cooperstown also benefits from the Hall of Fame, with several well-attended baseball camps located in the county. Youngsters from across the country attend these camps to take their best shot at the field of dreams. Similarly, the world-class opera house Glimmerglass, just outside Cooperstown, and the Foothills Performing Arts Center in Oneonta are both big cultural draws, augmenting tourism for the region.

For over two centuries Otsego County has been an agricultural hub, and while the number of farms is down significantly over the past hundred years, there is still a good number left and cause for optimism, for two reasons. First, the highly successful Greek yogurt company Chobani is headquartered about thirty minutes away from Oneonta, helping strengthen the agricultural sector of the local economy. Second, hops growing is making a comeback in the area. At one time, Otsego County was the center of hops growing for the entire country, until a blight hit in the early 1900s. Now that hops farming is returning, new craft breweries are being started, including the very successful Ommegang. Ommegang has also started sponsoring concerts in the summer, drawing respectable numbers and further strengthening the tourist industry. The major insurance company Central Mutual employs over nine hundred people in a remote part of rural Otsego County and continues to flourish, providing many jobs for locals.

Also, essential to the local economy, Otsego County is proud to have two fine institutions of higher learning—the State University of New York (SUNY) at Oneonta, and Hartwick College. These institutions employ thousands of people and aid in the upward mobility of many local residents and beyond. Among those who benefit are employees of Springbrook, a wonderful institution dedicated to helping those with intellectual and developmental disabilities, ensuring that they live flourishing lives to the best of their potential. Springbrook employs close to a thousand people and has a cooperative program with SUNY Oneonta that enables their employees to earn degrees with the university. From the northern side of Otsego County, the commute to the nearby cities of Utica and Rome is only about thirty minutes, and the county hopes to benefit by the spike in nanotechnology investments and manufacturing activities in those areas, which brings the promise of new high-tech jobs to the region.

In addition to Ioxus, Oneonta is home to other manufacturing firms, including a contingent of the Corning corporation with more than two hundred employees, and Custom Electronics. Otsego County is working on its airport, expanding the runway and support operations to facilitate the economic growth throughout the region. The Oneonta Job Corps Academy played a pivotal role in helping the airport modernize its facilities. In the Congress, I was proud to be the Republican cochair of the Job Corps Congressional Caucus. This program helps young Americans get a second chance in life by preparing them for career and technical jobs across a wide variety of professions and occupations. Supporting all of these activities in rural Otsego County are many small businesses (including the famous Brooks BBQ), secondary schools for children, and health care industries, including Bassett Medical Center and supporting clinics, which are pervasive in the region.

A Twenty-First-Century Economy

Otsego County, like the rest of America, needs help. We need reforms to help our economy grow so that our citizens can see rising wages and enjoy a flourishing life. With unified Republican Party control of the federal government, there is the opportunity to get this done.

Here's my list of recommended policy changes to promote a thriving twenty-first-century economy.

1. Reform the tax code. Our present code is antigrowth, complex, and unfair to ordinary Americans who can't afford a lobbyist to help secure carve-outs. The last time we enacted major tax reform was 1986. Today, there are special carve-outs everywhere.

Indeed, while the U.S. government takes in over $3.3 trillion a year, it leaves on the table over $1.3 trillion in so-called tax expenditures (loopholes) every year. We need to go through the code, closing loopholes (like the Wall Street carve-out for "carried interest" and other protections for special interests) so that we can lower rates and help close the deficit. This will spur growth in the economy because small businesses will have more money to invest (in new capital projects and additional hires). Tax reform will also increase middle-class consumption. Given that two-thirds of our economy is consumer spending–driven and that middle-class Americans historically spend 96 percent of their take-home pay, tax reform that puts more in the pocket of ordinary Americans is sure to grow the economy, ultimately bringing in more revenues to the treasury, helping us get back to a balanced budget. Tax reform should be comprehensive, dealing with both individual and business codes. Our business tax rate, approaching 40 percent (when the federal and state tax burden is combined), is the highest in the world, hurting our competitiveness and causing distortions in the market as companies find overseas shelters to lower their overall tax burden.

2. Reform regulations. Start with the REINS Act. The legislative branch needs to reclaim its Article I powers and exercise oversight of the executive branch. Federal regulations cost the U.S. economy over $2 trillion a year. Federal regulations are often onerous and duplicate state regulations. We desperately need reform.

3. Revitalize infrastructure. A world-class economy requires world-class infrastructure. In the Congress, I was an original cosponsor of Representative John Delaney's Partnership to Build America Act, which linked business tax reform with infrastructure improvements to spur significant economic growth. This bill was designed to incentivize the movement of corporate assets held in overseas accounts back to the United States and into major infrastructure projects (roads, bridges, water, sewer, broadband expansion, renewable energy, and so on). Utilizing a "reverse Dutch auction" and a tax rate of 8 percent instead of the 35 percent in current law, we anticipated that this could draw as much as $50 billion of overseas corporate money into the infrastructure market, a transformative number that would recapitalize and significantly expand our assets. For all that needed investment, the cost to the taxpayer would be zero. This would be entirely private money helping finance major infrastructure projects.

This bill will not only revitalize our infrastructure and reform the business tax code, but also put construction companies, contractors, and hardworking laborers to work. For the Republican Party, this bill will help solidify the pivotal 2016 Rust Belt voting coalition.

As part of our infrastructure revitalization program, we should also take action to help convert our existing brownfields. As the economy transformed from the industrial to the information age, many manufacturing companies moved or closed, leaving massive structures behind, often with asbestos or other hazardous materials inside. Unfortunately, these decrepit structures still remain today. I teamed up with Democratic representative Elizabeth Esty from Connecticut to offer a bill that reauthorized the tax incentive to clean up and transform these brownfield sites. In my congressional district, we had the old Beech-Nut nutrition and chewing gum company factory in Canajoharie, Montgomery County. In its heyday, this site employed thousands of people and was the major driver of the local economy. Employment at the site significantly declined over the years, and the company left the town completely about a decade ago. In the process, they left a facility that would become a serious environmental challenge requiring asbestos and black mold remediation. That blight detracts from an otherwise quaintly historic and attractive village along the Mohawk River and Interstate 90. This industrial site is also a significant safety hazard and must be remediated. Once cleaned up, it will be prime real estate for other promising economic development projects. Montgomery County executive Matt Ossenfort is working this issue to gain support from federal and state leadership, and passage of Esty-Gibson should be part of that effort. This initiative fits squarely within President Trump's campaign pledges and will also help our inner cities as they strive for revitalization.

4. Improve the health care system. We need a new health care system that provides quality care and more choices for consumers while reducing the costs. The 115th Congress is struggling with this issue now. The Affordable Care Act (also known as Obamacare) has left a trail of broken promises. While some Americans were helped, many were hurt by significantly higher costs, eroded quality, and fewer choices.

Obamacare has also wreaked havoc on small businesses. One of the many examples in my district was Schmidt's Wholesale in Monticello, Sullivan County. Chris Schmidt is the third-generation executive for this family-owned business of about fifty people. Chris's grandfather and father had always covered 100 percent of all health care costs for their employees. When I visited with Chris in 2013, he was very emotional, explaining, with his books in front of him, how he tried everything possible to continue that traditional standard, but with health care costs increasing by over 20 percent annually, he was forced to make his employees contribute to their health care. He felt he was letting his family down, but saw no other choice. There has got to be a better way.

President Trump has vowed to repeal and replace Obamacare.

Republicans in Congress agree with that concept. In theory, repealing is the easier part. Utilizing the parliamentary maneuver of budget reconciliation, the same technique that was employed to pass it, Congress should be able to get rid of the most oner-ous sections of this law fairly quickly, since that will only require fifty-one votes in the Senate (not the filibuster threshold of sixty). Working the fine-point policy details and garnering enough bipartisan votes for the replacement will be harder. These two bills should be voted on the same day after a bipartisan agreement is reached on the replacement. The repeal vote should come first.

The health care plan that I have supported includes some parts of Obamacare—coverage for those with preexisting condi-tions, protections against losing coverage when sick, and allow-ing parents to keep their children on health care plans until they are twenty-six years old. Beyond that, we should move the loci of power from government-controlled co-ops and mandates to patient-centered reforms that empower citizens to decide and man-age their own care. These reforms should include expanded nontax-able health savings accounts and inject more choice by eliminating the exemption health care insurance companies enjoy so that they get monopolies inside state lines. That change will allow Americans to shop countrywide for their plan. Competition will help drive down prices while retaining quality. To help lower-income fami-lies, we should provide subsidies to help them purchase a compet-itive plan in the marketplace, and there should be an affordable catastrophic coverage option for young folks.

This replacement plan should also include tort reform to help drive down overall costs, using the successful model enacted in California. If enacted, this reform should both reduce cost and inspire more people to become doctors. Considering basic supply and demand analysis, having more doctors should lower costs. Also on cost, Republicans should adopt the Democratic Party idea of competitive bidding for prescription drugs. All of these provisions should help bend down the cost curve, while empowering people to manage their own health care plans and decisions.

Managing expectations will be important. Just as we had significant issues with health care before Obamacare, we can expect challenges after it is replaced. While that reality poses some political peril, it does not take away from the call to duty to do better than Obamacare. The American people are counting on us. Let's get this done right.

Regardless of where one comes down on Obamacare, we can all agree that if we keep people healthier longer, we not only improve quality of life, but we also drive down costs. That was the impetus for the landmark legislation H.R. 6, 21st Century Cures, which I played a role in authoring, and which was enacted at the close of the 114th Congress. This bill provides close to $5 billion in new investments in health care research and portends good news for Americans suffering from cancer, heart disease, or Alzheimer's, as well as those on the autism spectrum, those addicted to opioids, those in need of mental health services, and, with the section that I authored for the bill, those exposed to chronic Lyme and other tick-borne diseases.

Over the years, tens of thousands of people in my area have suffered tick bites and been afflicted with pernicious diseases like Lyme and other coinfections such as babesiosis and anaplasmosis. If these diseases are left untreated or improperly treated, many sufferers endure chronic illness and may lack adequate insurance company coverage as they deal with these challenges. The provisions enacted in 21st Century Cures give them a fighting chance.

In addition to increasing investments in medical research, this bill brings two other major reforms. First, it changes the way we share information. The majority of the regulatory state was established before the information age and before we had such technologies as portals and the cloud. As such, much stovepiping exists, limiting collaborative activity among researchers. The 21st Century Cures legislation makes better use of technology, facilitating sharing among researchers and bringing patients into the process, making it easier for them to volunteer for aggressive clinical trials when diagnosed with a life-threatening disease. The synergy from these changes should help us bring forward cures and solutions more quickly. Likewise, the other major move in this bill makes it easier and faster to bring to market curative drugs and medical devices. It should not take up to twelve years to make these life-saving and life-enhancing products available for consumers.

Another factor is that this is a highly competitive global market and, candidly, with current restrictions, we are losing competitiveness in the medical research space. Thus not only are Americans suffering longer while waiting on our regulatory state, but we are also losing drug development research jobs to Europe, where the industry is much more agile. We sorely needed this reform, and its enactment in the 114th Congress marks a significant achievement for House Energy and Commerce chairman Fred Upton, the entire committee on both sides of Capitol Hill, and the Obama administration. It is also good news for the American people. How this bill was crafted is a great example of constituent-driven legislation.

5. Prepare our workers. In addition, we need *education reform* that helps empower local schools and supports career technical education to prepare Americans to contribute to the twenty-first-century economy. Companies like Ioxus and Amphenol are counting on us to get that done. Education reform will help strengthen equal opportunity and upward mobility for all citizens, supporting working families and businesses.

In 2014, Congress enacted the Skills Act, which helps prepare workers to enter building construction and technical trades positions. In 2015, we repealed and replaced President George W. Bush's No Child Left Behind with the Every Student Succeeds Act (ESSA). The act sends power back to the states and local school districts, allows states to withdraw from Common Core without penalty, ends the high-stakes portion of federal testing, invests in teacher mentorship, and gives school districts more flexibility in spending federal resources. All of these initiatives are steps in the right direction. Additionally, in the 114th Congress, the U.S. House passed a reauthorization of the Perkins Act, legislation to further help career and technical worker preparation, but unfortunately it was not considered in the Senate. The 115th Congress should enact it.

Lastly, I support charter schools in circumstances where their creation will not adversely impact public schools, and voucher programs for parochial education. We can improve our public schools while also supporting choice. In the end, the focus is on students, helping them prepare to be successful in the twenty-first-century economy and to live a flourishing life.

6. Emphasize fair trade. Trade is essential for the U.S. economy. In my district, it impacts across the economy—on the dairy industry, defense companies like Amphenol, and small high-tech companies like Ioxus. We must stop making bad trade agreements. Massive multilateral trade deals like NAFTA have not been good for this country. They create competitive disadvantages for our companies, causing much of our manufacturing base to move overseas. Going forward, we should focus on bilateral agreements that make sure our negotiators can pin down issues and secure stipulations that ensure our companies and workers are on a level playing field with our global competitors. Our first move should be to scrap TPP and sit down directly with the Chinese to secure a bilateral agreement that addresses trade, currency manipulation, intellectual property rights, and national security. It's in both our interests to do so.

7. Become an energy exporter. We should become energy independent and continue on course to be the world's largest exporter of energy. I'm a firm believer that we can simultaneously lead the world in energy production and be a leader on the environment. If we operate smartly, we don't have to choose between these competing priorities. Growing up in a working-class family that got crushed by the spiking gas and home heating prices of the 1970s, I know firsthand how critical this issue is for the American people. Those price increases directly impacted our quality of life. Every extra dollar on gas and home heating was one less available for any other priority. Conversely, when gas prices dropped from their height of over $4 a gallon to a little over $2 a gallon for much of my time in Congress, that was like a tax cut for working-class Americans. The same goes for home heating costs, which have also declined. At the federal and state level, we should be doing what we can to expand supply to ensure we keep these prices as low as possible. When working-class people have more disposal income, they tend to spend it locally, which increases the velocity of money, growing the local economy, which helps produce revenues for local government, helping balance budgets.

A comprehensive "all of the above" energy approach has not only helped the American people, it has also reduced greenhouse gas emissions, improving the quality of our environment. Based on a 2005 benchmark, we have reduced emissions by over

15 percent nationally, a result of cleaner coal (via scrubbers and low-sulfur approaches), increased use of natural gas, continued use of nuclear power, and increases in solar, wind, hydroelectricity, geothermal, and other clean and renewable energy sources. Energy efficiency has also improved, positively impacting the energy market and contributing to a cleaner environment. After all, a kilowatt saved is equivalent to a kilowatt produced. It is very important that we keep a balanced approach to these competing priorities going forward. If we get this wrong in either direction, we put our country at peril, adversely impacting working-class Americans and small businesses with burdensome higher energy costs on the one end, and potentially altering the environment in ways that put future generations at risk on the other. We must get the judgment right.

There are ways we can employ technology, with proper and helpful regulation, to capture methane and mitigate risk to deliver natural gas safely to local businesses and consumers. We must insist on that standard. Gas companies should be complying with the Safe Drinking Water Act and disclosing chemicals. These increased standards will provide safeguards to ensure we keep our air and water protected. Once we do that, and enhance safety, we will benefit from a wider use of an energy source that is cleaner and cheaper than other fossil fuels. Natural gas will be part of a comprehensive energy strategy that provides safe, cheaper, and cleaner energy for all Americans.

8. Restore the dignity of work. To help create jobs, boost wages, and ensure that all Americans have the opportunity to rise to their God-given potential, we will also need to reform the welfare system. Consider this: A person collecting unemployment may get as much as $400 a week, while a person working for minimum wage makes $290 a week. You can make more by staying home than by toiling in the fields of a farm. How did we let that happen?

As we work to rectify that situation, to help incentivize workers to stay in the workforce instead of making more by collecting unemployment, I support expanding the Earned Income Tax Credit (EITC). I saw firsthand with my dad how important work was for his dignity. Let's ensure our policies reflect that priority.

By executive order, President Obama overturned President Clinton's reforms to the welfare system that required work for recipients. The Clinton-era work requirements must be restored. The welfare state was always intended to be a temporary hand up to Americans down on their luck for one reason or another, as they ultimately pursue the American dream. Too many are now trapped in a cycle of welfare and poverty. Addressing that is as much a moral imperative as it is an economic one. Every American has special gifts and natural rights, and among those is a flourishing life. By transitioning Americans back to work and helping promote rising wages for working-class people, we will help restore dignity, strengthen the American dream, and lift up this nation.

9. Promote sustainability. We must get back to a balanced budget. Working together over the past six years, we cut the deficit by over two-thirds, but we must continue on that path until we achieve balance. Our policies must be sustainable. The Republican Party has always been the leader on fiscal responsibility, and the American people are counting on us to get this done. An integral component of the American dream is to work hard so that our children have a better life and more opportunity than we did. With continued deficits and a mounting debt, we are in jeopardy of failing them.

The first step is to *enact the pro-growth policy recommendations* already mentioned. Quite frankly, given the financial commitments we have made to retirees and those requiring safety net assistance, and the revenues needed to pay for national defense, infrastructure, education, and other requirements in the federal departments, the fact is that *our economy simply must grow at 4 percent in GDP* to enable us to pay our bills. If we don't grow at that rate, we won't bring in enough revenues to balance the budget, even after budget reforms. Thus pro-growth policies should not be a partisan issue— they are essential for our cherished way of life.

In addition to pro-growth reforms, we must take steps to ensure that our spending levels are sustainable. That was so important to me that I supported the *Cooper-LaTourette budget* proposal that was inspired by the Simpson-Bowles commission. That budget promoted growth in the economy and targeted spending levels for discretionary and mandatory spending programs to guide us back to a balanced budget.

We are long overdue to enact a *balanced budget amendment to the Constitution*. There are several versions of this policy reform, with strong arguments for each. We should pick the one with the most political support and advance it. An exception for emergencies such as time of war or natural disaster will naturally be required.

We must take action to ensure that the programs that support senior citizens remain viable, now and in the future. On the current path, both Social Security and Medicare will go bankrupt in the next few decades, jeopardizing our solemn pledges to our seniors. As a people, we keep our promises, and this is a serious test for our generation—will we be up to the task of mandatory spending reform to ensure we keep our word for future generations?

Fortunately, there is a path forward to save both of these programs. For Medicare, there is the Medicare Advantage program, where seniors choose a health insurance plan from among several competing insurance companies, and once they have selected one, the government pays the premium, allowing seniors to manage their own health care. This voluntary program, about a decade old, has already saved the taxpayer a significant amount of money, while increasing customer satisfaction. Today over one-third of my constituents are on this program. The Democratic Party for several election cycles claimed that this "Ryan Plan" ends Medicare as we know it. That's completely false, and in fact, this false claim was selected as the "lie of the year" by the nonpartisan website Politifact. Moreover, this bogus claim denies the reality that seniors are increasingly voluntarily entering the program.

To depoliticize this issue and save Medicare, I recommend that we continue to incentivize and support the voluntary expansion of Medicare Advantage. Coupling that initiative, along with changing the policy to allow Medicare to competitively bid for prescription drugs, will bend down the cost curve and push solvency for Medicare out another decade into the 2040s, when Baby Boomer demographic pressures begin to ease. With just these two tweaks, we can save Medicare.

Social Security solvency is jeopardized starting in 2035, according to latest actuarial estimates. According to the Social Security Administration, in that year, if reforms are not enacted, benefits will need to be reduced to 75 percent of their full levels. Given that one-third of all seniors in this country live on only their Social Security check, we simply cannot allow that to happen. Fortunately, with only minor reforms, we can ensure 100 percent benefits for all current and future seniors. The latest health studies conclude that seniors who are wealthy are living on average twelve years longer than their peers with more modest incomes. Given that fact, current Social Security projections on life expectancy and corresponding contribution requirements should be readjusted. With these minor modifications, we will preserve both of these sacred programs for future generations and help us get back to a balanced budget—a fiscal and moral imperative.

Saving Capitalism

There is a restlessness in the land. The results of the 2016 presidential election certainly validated this point. Americans feel that their country is out of control and rudderless, without vision for the future. In this chapter, I've argued for a balanced approach, focused on promoting a flourishing life for all Americans.

From a close reading of history, we can gain insights. First, for all its challenges and pitfalls, *no system has produced more freedom and prosperity than capitalism.* The social movement on the American left wants to discard it for socialism. They may have good intentions, but this would be a colossal mistake. Socialism will not produce wealth, and it will certainly curtail freedom, opportunity, and upward mobility. To embrace socialism would be to accept defeat and proclaim the American dream dead. U.S. senator Bernie Sanders has a large, faithful following. It consists of Americans who want the best for our country and a fairer distribution of its wealth. As conservatives, we too want what's best for this country, and we agree that workers' wages and quality of life have been stagnating for too long. It is incumbent on us to convince Americans (including the left) that we can achieve these mutually desired goals by *reforming our political system and strengthening capitalism.*

At the end of the day, we are still better off with the Locke-Rousseau hybrid that balances the individual with the family/

community than the Hegelian, statist approach that counts on big government to solve everything. Our founding principles were different from Europe by conscious design, and the reasons for those are as relevant today as they were back in the eighteenth century.

At the same time, let's recognize that the Locke-Rousseau hybrid is in trouble. We are out of balance. Greed is an issue in our society. Although it is not representative of the majority of American companies, when we have some corporate CEOs making hundreds of millions of dollars while their entry-level employees are on government assistance (which "we the people" pay for), we have a problem. CEOs are responsible for their company's performance. They must be successful or the company will fail and go bankrupt. That is the responsibility of leadership in a capitalistic society, and for taking on those burdens and high responsibility, *they should be paid handsomely.* At the same time, CEOs are also responsible for treating their employees fairly, commensurate with their contributions to the team. When employees do their part and produce enormous earnings for shareholders and exorbitantly paid corporate executives, and these leaders in turn pass off the responsibility to financially provide for their workers to "we the people" (in the form of food stamps and heating assistance), that is wrong. It is also a big part of the reason why so many feel this system is rigged. Middle-class workers get stiffed, footing the bill for excessive executive compensation.

Let's change that. For companies presently falling into that category, if they increase the pay of their workers to get them above federal welfare standards, I have no problem with them keeping the same compensation levels. This is not about taking money away from executives. It's about executives taking exorbitant compensation packages and then expecting the taxpayer to pay to get their workers above the welfare line.

Appealing to these executives' desire for public approbation and respect, not legislation, is probably the best course of action to get this done, for the same reason that James Madison argued that "extending the sphere" was the best way to attenuate the effects of special interests. We don't want the cure to be worse than the disease. Government should not legislate solutions for income inequality and corporate greed, but "we the people" can withhold our respect for those who take advantage of our fellow citizens. That action is shameful.

As Americans, we believe that the Creator endowed us with the natural right to a flourishing life. The American dream has been a hallmark achievement for our country—one that we as a people hold dear. The significant political upheaval observed in both major political parties right now is a direct result of a fraying of the American dream. Too many Americans no longer believe their success is up to them. They feel trapped in a rigged system where elites set the rules for their own gain at the expense of the rest of us. This has gone on for too long. It threatens the viability of our republic. If we are to live up to our founding principles, significant reform is required to promote a flourishing life. Dairy farmers like the Oomses, fruit and vegetable farmers like the Shutes, and companies like Amphenol and Ioxis are counting on us.

CHAPTER 4

Keep Faith

"You Gotta Believe"

I turned nine years old in 1973. Although I was raised Catholic with a strong belief in God, in a real sense my first personal experience with faith actually came through the game of baseball that season. That was the year my beloved New York Mets made the climb out of last place in the National League East in mid-August to ultimately overcome the St. Louis Cardinals during the last week of the season, backing into the pennant playoff series despite finishing with a mediocre 82–79 record.

In baseball, the pitcher who is brought in to get the last few outs for the team that is ahead in the game is called the closer. It's a high-pressure responsibility. Every time a closer is put in the game, they have to be at their best, with the outcome of the game literally riding on his performance. The Mets' closer in 1973 was Frank "Tug" McGraw. McGraw was a charismatic if somewhat quirky personality, who fit in perfectly with the demanding fans and challenging media market of New York. Undaunted, and ever the optimist, when asked in early September about the Mets' playoff prospects, the "Tugger," as he was known by all, proclaimed loud and proud, "You gotta believe!" It was quite a statement for a team that only a few days earlier was in last place in the division. That battle cry electrified Mets fans and the team. Soon thereafter, handmade posters plastered with that bold and hopeful statement popped up around the greater metropolitan area and populated every corner of Shea Stadium, the home field of the Mets. McGraw's optimism was infectious. The Mets' winning streak continued over the next few weeks and all of a sudden, incredibly, they looked like a team of destiny.

It was a special year I will never forget. Although I had lived in the small village of Kinderhook in upstate New York since 1968, our extended family on both sides still mostly lived in Long Island and New York City. To give my parents a break, for several weeks each summer I would be farmed out to my grandparents in Baldwin and Valley Stream on Long Island. In 1973, that occurred during the month of August, after Little League season was over and before school started again after Labor Day. In Baldwin there were children around my age who helped keep me entertained, but when I was transferred to Valley Stream about ten days in, time immediately began to stand still. My grandmother and great-aunt were glued to the TV, watching the Watergate hearings. I wasn't sure what to make of all that, but I somehow sensed it wasn't good. Aunt Fran used to talk under her breath about that "no-good Nixon."

I was surprised to hear adults talk badly about the president. Before then, in school and at home, the presidents I learned about were always viewed favorably, like the first president, the father of our nation, George Washington, the president who freed the slaves, Abraham Lincoln, the president who saved us from the Depression, FDR, and even the president who came from my little village—Martin Van Buren. I can't remember anyone talking badly about a president until Nixon, and I got no enjoyment at all watching the Watergate hearings. I needed a distraction, and candidly, I wanted something positive, something to believe in.

That's when it came. To my surprise and delight, all of a sudden the Mets were winning baseball games. The family didn't have air-conditioning back then, but the sweltering heat never bothered me when the TV was tuned to the Mets game. Like many Mets fans, I was mesmerized by the voices of our announcers—Ralph Kiner, Bob Murphy, and Lindsey Nelson. Everything seemed new and exciting, and I even had the opportunity to see a game live when my great-uncle Bill Gibson, the ticket manager for the Mets back then, took me to work one day. It was magical to be there in person. Everything was awesome: the players, the hot dogs, the vendors with their catchy sales pitches—even the grass. I remember thinking, "How did they get the grass on the field to look so green?"

When Labor Day rolled around, it was time to return to Kinderhook for the start of school, but when I got home, all I could talk about with family and friends was baseball and the Mets. Those were the days before cable, so unlike in Long Island where you could watch the Mets on a daily basis, back in Kinderhook we could only see them occasionally on Saturdays, when they were the game of the week. So to fill that hole and allow me to continue to follow the Mets' playoff run, Mom surprised me with a brand-new radio the first week of school. That radio was always tuned to an AM station that covered the Mets. When the game wasn't on, they often had sports commentators who analyzed every aspect of the previous game and what to expect in the next.

When the day finally came when we clinched the NL East, the headline in one of the New York papers the next day angered me. It was a quote from the manager of the National League West champions, the Cincinnati Reds, Sparky Anderson, and it read, "Don't Tell Yogi [Yogi Berra was the Mets' manager], but This Won't Be a Series." The Reds had won 99 baseball games that year and were heavily favored to win the pennant series. No one conveyed that message to the Mets, however—they were ready to play baseball—and their fans' faith only intensified after Anderson's dismissive comments. Had Twitter existed in 1973, I'm convinced the hashtag #YouGottaBelieve would have been the leading trend that fall.

It was an incredible series that went all five games before the Mets prevailed. As if right from a Hollywood script, our closer, Tug McGraw, was brought in in the ninth inning to complete the destruction of the "Big Red Machine." He retired both batters he faced. It was official, the Mets were going to the World Series—David had slain Goliath. To my obviously biased perspective, the good guys had won. We seemed destined to win the World Series. We had faith God would make it so. "You gotta believe!" We were ready for the Oakland Athletics.

It turned out to be an odd series, for a variety of reasons. First, just having the Mets in it was odd. To this day, they hold the record of the lowest regular-season winning percentage of any team to make it to the World Series. Their competitors, the Oakland A's, were pure spectacle. Their colorful uniforms (that's about as kind of a description you'll ever hear) combining pastel green and bright yellow were only surpassed in boldness by the personality of the A's owner himself, the ostentatious Chuck Finley. Finley even made headlines himself after game 2, when he put his second baseman Mike Andrews on the disabled list after Andrews made two errors in the twelfth inning, costing the A's that game. The A's players protested that vindictive move, which MLB commissioner Bowie Kuhn ultimately overturned to protect the integrity of the game. Years later we learned that had

Kuhn not invalidated Finley's decision, the A's baseball players would not have taken to the field in game 3, which would have made the Mets World Series champions by default.

For their part, the A's players reflected the rebel streak of their owner, a number of them sporting showy handlebar mustaches and groovy haircuts. It was definitely the 1970s. Even the A's stadium made headlines. On sunny autumn afternoons, given the angle of the field and the stadium's construction, it was very difficult to catch fly balls—outfielders were literally blinded by the light. Left field was called the "sun field" for that reason, and indeed, that would play a factor in this fall classic. Willie Mays, a transformative figure in baseball, was playing in his last games ever, wearing a Mets uniform. The Mets right fielder, Rusty Staub, would defy doctors and play through a painful and debilitating injury to his shoulder, turning in star performances, such as in game 4, when he had multiple hits and RBIs, including a decisive three-run home run. Meanwhile, all this played out against the backdrop of Tug McGraw and the "You gotta believe" Mets striving to claim their rightful destiny as world champions.

After the teams split the first two games in Oakland, the series moved back to New York for game 3. I learned that Uncle Bill had secured two tickets for us to attend the game. I couldn't believe it—I was going to attend a World Series game! Then my dad broke the news: "I have to work that day." He planned to give the tickets to our priest, Father John Caldera. I was devastated. To this day, I have the image of Father Caldera parking his Cadillac in our driveway, walking up to our stoop wearing black pants and a white T-shirt, where he was met by Dad. They talked briefly as I prayed Dad would change his mind. Then it happened—my dad handed over the tickets. I held that against Father Caldera for years, although clearly it was not his fault. We lost game 3. Then won games 4 and 5. The emotional roller coaster was dizzying, but at last we seemed poised to win it all. There were the details of flying back to Oakland where the series would finish, but after all, we only had to win one of the next two games, and we had our aces, Tom Seaver and Jon Matlack, scheduled to pitch those games. It all seemed clinched. Then Seaver and the Mets lost game 6. As mentally and physically tough as he was—Seaver went all eight innings—he simply got outpitched. Still, there was game 7, and the Mets seemed destined to win that game. We believed it would happen, and we had faith in God's plan.

Alas, it did not start well. With one out in the third inning, Oakland A's pitcher Ken Holtzman doubled. The designated-hitter rule had just been implemented that year in the American League, and accordingly, Holtzman did not have a single at bat during the regular season, making his double off one of the best pitchers in baseball all the more impressive. The A's shortstop, Bert Campaneris, then stepped up to the plate. He was not considered a long-ball threat at all, having hit only two home runs the entire year. In fact, it was game 7 and the A's hadn't hit a single home run the entire series. Until Campaneris did, a two-run blast. I couldn't believe it. Campaneris didn't hit home runs. How could that happen? In the Gibson household, things were not going well. I started carrying on, making quite a scene. It didn't get any better when a few batters later, A's slugger Reggie Jackson hit another two-run homer. The A's were up 4–0. My complaining got worse and Dad put me on notice. He lectured me that there was more to life than just baseball and that if my bad behavior continued, I would be sent to my room. More to life than baseball? Wasn't possible. Sent to my room during game 7 of the World Series? Dad was strict, but surely he would never do that.

You can see where this is heading. In the fifth inning, the A's added another run off an RBI single by left fielder Joe Rudi. I immediately started complaining, and that's when my father ejected me from the game. He sent me to my room. I spent the next hour or so alternating between cupping my hand against the door to hear the game better and crying on my bed. The Mets lost game 7. I was beyond sad; nothing in the world seemed to make sense. For the past two months, everything in my life had centered on the Mets. We were the team of destiny. Tug McGraw had inspired us to believe, and we did. It had carried us to the World Series despite the obvious shortcomings of our team. Baseball seemed to trump politics and everything else. Who cared about Watergate with the Mets winning the World Series?

Yet it wasn't to be and I was left to put the pieces together. I had kept the faith and ended up crushed. There seemed to be no justice in the world and the pain was unbearable.

As it turned out, however, my real problem was that I didn't know anything at all about actual pain and heartbreak. I thought I did when we lost game 7, but I was only nine years old, and I was wrong about that, too.

I found out a few years later when my paternal grandfather died. Grandpa Gibson was the first death I experienced of someone I loved. I felt that loss deeply. Losing the World Series wasn't even in the same league. Baseball was important, but it wasn't the most important thing in life.

That baseball season provided important life lessons. It went much beyond baseball, incorporating politics, faith, religion, and philosophy en route to the first crushing defeat I ever experienced.

I was starting to appreciate where faith and free will intersected. It was important to believe in a cause, but God's work is not to make it so—that depends on us. By creating us, God makes things possible. After that, it's up to us, and success depends on hard work, determination, skill, teamwork, and a healthy dose of luck. It was painful to learn it by watching the Mets lose, but I'm better for it. As much as I hate losing anything, to this day I must admit—sometimes we learn more in defeat. In 1973, my experiences with real ups and downs was just beginning, but even now, whenever I'm asked to have faith in something—a new political perspective, a policy position—I think of Tugger and my experience believing in a team that probably shouldn't have made the World Series but did.

I have one final postscript about the 1973 Mets. Years later, when country singer Tim McGraw released his big hit "Live Like You Were Dying," a touching tribute to his dad, the great Tug McGraw, as he was losing his life to cancer, all of those memories of that special season when I was nine years old came flooding back to me.

It was the spring of 2005, and I was redeploying from Iraq. McGraw's song was getting a lot of airtime and it was a very difficult period—we had lost Wobler and Pusateri on that deployment. Dad was right, of course, there was more to life than baseball. Yet even though it is just a game, in some ways baseball is transformative and larger than life in how it excites, challenges, and unites people across generations and among every imaginable background with experiences of incredible triumph and crushing defeat, and at times redemption. Tug McGraw fathered Tim out of wedlock and denied paternity for years before fully embracing his son when Tim was seventeen years old. They went on to have a very close relationship until Tug's death. In the end, it was a beautiful story of redemption, validated by Tim's moving song of remembrance. Poignantly, as Tim McGraw's music video concludes, there is footage of the Tugger throwing the final pitch, striking out Kansas City Royals batter Willie Wilson, to win the 1980 World Series. Sure, McGraw is wearing a Philadelphia Phillies uniform in that scene, but for me those are minor details, because what I see is a dynamic young pitcher in New York Mets pinstripes calling me to believe. I'm answering him back, "I do believe," and I've kept the faith ever since. Thanks, Tug McGraw.

Faith and the Existential Question—Why Are We Here on Earth?

Religious faith is an important component of American life. That was so for our very first settlers in the early seventeenth century and remains the case for most Americans today. We established a government with the citizen in charge to secure our rights, including religious liberty. All Americans have freedom of religion—to worship God as they are called—or not to believe at all. We have the choice.

Many of us believe that God created us in His own image, with our own originality reflected in the soul. While we have tolerance for all religions, we are especially moved by the moral code of conduct in the Judeo-Christian faiths as described in the Old and New Testaments of the Bible. Christians find inspiration in the personal example of Jesus Christ. The way He lived His life provides example for our conduct here on earth, and His sacrifice provides hope for eternal life after our human demise.

Putting emphasis on conduct assumes that we freely make choices. Indeed, free will figures prominently in theology, philosophy, and politics, from which the principle of *personal responsibility* logically follows, so essential to any political system formulated on the rule of law.

As we contemplate conduct, we remember Jesus's commandment to love one another. Jesus said that whenever you love another, you are loving Him. In the Old Testament, the Ten Commandments inform our code of conduct, teaching us to be honest, trustworthy, not steal or commit murder, and to honor God, our parents, and the Sabbath. Jesus helped us prioritize, clearly placing love above all. As conservatives, we must remember that. At times our strong faith may tempt us to judge rather than love, which can alienate us from Jesus and our fellow citizens, weakening our movement and the republic. As we unify and grow the conservative movement, this is essential. Remember, as the song says, "They will know we are Christians by our love."

Faith and love help organize and inform our lives, making us good citizens. Our unique American political culture that establishes a competitive meritocracy in our economic lives relies on a citizen with a kind heart in our private lives, caring deeply about family, friends, and community. Religious faith informs those duties and responsibilities, and when citizens widely practice this, we are a better nation.

Living one's life in a moral and just way can also enhance individual happiness. God outfits us with emotions to help us make good decisions—to freely and selflessly love one another. Think about the last time you did something good for someone else. When you made a choice, freely, to do something for someone else purely for the sake of serving another—remember the feeling you had? There is a description for the warm feeling you get when you do something selfless—it's euphoria or ecstasy. One translation of ecstasy is *rapturous delight* or *connection with God*. When we love another, we make a connection with God. We are naturally outfitted to be rewarded with euphoria when we follow Jesus's first commandment.

As you read this you may be thinking of your own experiences of being intrinsically rewarded for kind and thoughtful behavior. I'll share one of mine. During redeployment from Iraq after the Persian Gulf War in 1991, my unit of the 82nd Airborne Division was flying from Kuwait back to Fort Bragg on a 747 jumbo jet commercial flight. The atmosphere on that flight was joyous and celebratory. The troops were heading home and couldn't wait. The stewardesses on board were very attentive—drinks and snacks were flowing. They also enjoyed the banter with soldiers who after eight months in the desert were eager for such interactions. It wasn't long before the first paratrooper took off the airborne wings from his uniform and presented it to one of the attractive young female flight attendants. This touched off a frenzy, with many paratroopers following suit. Before long, all of the beautiful stewardesses were proudly showing off these nice souvenirs, which now adorned their own uniforms.

As I watched this unfold, I noticed that one of the hardest-working attendants, who looked to be in her early sixties, was being totally ignored. She was very aware of what was going on, as at one point one of her colleagues stopped to show her the airborne wings she had received. This mature flight attendant congratulated her associate and went back to work, diligently moving about the cabin in search of any trooper needing service. It didn't seem right. More than anyone, she deserved recognition. I decided to give her something special that no other stewardess had received. I took out my Swiss Army knife and cut off my Ranger Tab from the upper left sleeve of my desert camouflage uniform. I waited patiently as she continued her rounds. When she got to me and asked if I needed anything, I turned and presented her with the Ranger Tab, expressing my gratitude for her dedicated work. I then explained the significance of the U.S. Army Ranger Tab. A big smile came to her face and she thanked me. She disappeared for a couple of minutes to get a safety pin and then returned with it attached to her uniform. She then went back to work, but with a new aura. She felt validated and appreciated. It made me feel really good, too.

It's been over twenty-six years since that flight, but I remember that emotional experience like it was yesterday. One postscript: As our flight was preparing to land in Rome, Italy, for refueling, that stewardess came and grabbed me by the hand. "Come with me," she said. I wasn't sure what was up, but it seemed harmless, and I went along. She took me to the pilot's cabin, where I was buckled into a seat with the pilots to see the incredible panoramic views of Rome as we landed at the international airport. I had been expecting nothing in return, but instead was filled with overwhelming happiness and an unforgettable image of Rome. God has created humans so that when we serve others, we receive more than we give. That was one of Mother Teresa's central messages in her inspirational life. Love and service are two acts where the reward can surpass the action.

When humans, exercising their free will, make the choice to love another, we are connected to God. In that way, we see the joining of the imperfect (human free will) with the perfect (God). That juxtaposition at once completes us as humans, and completes God, providing illumination of God's perfection in His joining with human imperfection. As humans, we possess rationality and free will. When we volitionally choose to love God, we fulfill our purpose—completing the universe—and that's why we are here on earth.

Our Soul and the Afterlife

I had a life-changing experience during the congressional delegation trip to Israel I led in the summer of 2016. We spent a few hours seeing the sights in Jerusalem, including the Church of the Holy Sepulchre, where Christians believe Jesus was crucified and buried. The church was built by Constantine, the first Roman emperor to embrace Jesus as his personal savior. He did so at the urging of his mother, Helen (later Saint Helen). At the church, we were able to see the site of Jesus's cross, where His body was prepared for burial, and where He was entombed. I had a moment of clarity that strengthened my faith. There was an overwhelming, powerful presence like no other I've experienced. Mary Jo and I were both much moved and emotional throughout our time at the church. This emotion is best described as *hope*. Absorbing the moment, I came to the belief that Jesus changed our understanding of this word. Through His personal example, His teaching, and ultimately His sacrifice, we came to fully appreciate hope—the possibility of eternal life by living in accordance with His teachings. Reflecting on that experience, I now see clearer the connection between how we exercise our free will, our soul's connection with God, and the path to Heaven. I also believe that forming a political system that maximizes *freedom* helps humans live flourishing lives in step with virtue and ultimately in union with God.

That life-changing experience helped me deal with the ordeal of Mom's death later that year. On her last day, our family had several precious hours with her before she lost consciousness. She interacted with us, sharing in many wonderful and funny memories. Later, while she was in hospice and preparing to leave this world for Heaven, I was overwhelmed again by the experience of hope—the image and extraordinary sense of the Church of the Holy Sepulchre. As we watched Mom take her last breath, I was very thankful for the meaningful and loving life she lived and the hope that Jesus gives us all. Watching my mom die, and experiencing how strong her faith was in facing those last moments, and feeling God's presence there with us, has strengthened my faith.

The Church of the Holy Sepulchre in Jerusalem.

We are never too old to learn, change, and improve. We are never beyond or without hope.

Getting It Right

With our faith-based system connecting human free will, individual conduct, and our relationship with God, it becomes readily apparent that faith has import beyond religion—it is also essential to civic life. Our Founders changed the trajectory of history when they established a self-governing republic with the citizen in charge. The form of government they established was decidedly liberal for the late eighteenth century—including the ratification

of a Bill of Rights for all citizens. This radical political arrangement stood in stark contrast to the prevailing political order in
which individuals were subjects of the crown, with no safeguards
for God-given natural rights, nor upward mobility to improve
their station in life. Without rights and without hope, such an
existence was not a flourishing life at all. Our Founders threw
off that system and established one based on liberty. Modern-day
conservatives seek to conserve those liberal principles, rejecting
the repressive approaches of the past and neostatist schemes of the
present. Keeping faith in founding principles is central for conservatives, because if we stop believing we can govern ourselves, then
nothing else we do from a political perspective matters.

Sometimes as conservatives we suffer unwittingly from mud-
dled thinking. Impressed by the writings of John Locke and
Adam Smith with their emphasis on the individual and related,
strong justifications for capitalism, we become uninformed consumers of radical empiricism and the moral relativism inherent in
unreconstructed Enlightenment thought. Among the Enlightenment ideas most problematic is the notion of "progress." Conservatives occasionally get trapped in the rush to put that ideal at the
pinnacle of American life. Indeed, even Ronald Reagan at times
invoked the ideal of progress. It is very alluring. As I established
earlier, we are all in pursuit of a "better self," so doesn't that validate the idea of "progress" as an unqualified virtuous quality? No,
not unqualified, anyway.

To be clear, commitment to excellence and constantly seeking
self-improvement are most certainly virtuous dispositions. Conservatives want all Americans to aspire to such a life as we as a
people strive to fully instantiate the ideals professed in our founding documents. Indeed, that was the point of Dr. King's speech
on the National Mall, where he called on us to be a country where

everyone could rise to their God-given potential and be judged on the content of their character. Such words and deeds are a great example of a liberty-minded people endeavoring to get it right. The same is true for the suffragettes of the nineteenth century and early twentieth century who petitioned to secure the right to vote for women. This is another excellent example of a liberty-inspired society moving toward its professed ideals—working to get it right. The efforts of advocates to this day to ensure that all people of this republic have equal opportunity, liberty, and equal protection under the law are entirely consistent with efforts to get it right.

We must delineate acts of self-improvement, however, from unadulterated, boundless adulation for the concept of "progress." The central problem with "progress" as an unquestioned and unqualified good is that it is at war with universals; it is at odds with the very idea that there is such a thing as "right" and "wrong." If *everything* is about progress, then nothing is perfect or true. The problem with unconditionally accepting "progress" is that it is the very definition of moral relativism. Moral relativism puts in jeopardy the whole project of the American founding, which was Aristotelian—about "getting it right."

The founding was also about accepting compromise and moderation so that we could escape violent change and replace it with peaceful, evolutionary change. There is a nuance here—our Founders promoted self-improvement, but they firmly believed that there was such a thing as universal right and wrong. It they didn't believe that, they wouldn't have published the Bill of Rights. As conservatives, we reject moral relativism and keep faith with founding principles and our desire to get it right.

Moral relativism has eroded the balance in our political culture and individual lives and partially explains the problems we're experiencing in American life today. When we celebrate the unbridled pursuit of individual happiness at the expense of family and community responsibilities because such actions are consonant with progress in a society that celebrates freedom, we evidence loss of balance in a republic that once was committed to getting that right. Pursuing one's dreams is absolutely consistent with life in a free society, but judgment matters; there is an appropriate point where if one continues seeking to maximize utility, forsaking all other commitments, one is not getting it right—just being selfish.

Conservative political thought starts with the Greek philosophers Socrates, Plato, and Aristotle. These figures surely had differences among them, some quite stark. Conservatives, for example, should shudder at the recommended political construction in Plato's *Republic* that severely restricted freedom and prescribed a heavy-handed government to rule over its subjects. Conservatives generally embrace Aristotle's construction of virtue as essential to citizenship and his advocacy for intellectual freedom. Aristotle maintained that virtue was the midpoint between extremes. Humans exercise judgment to discern among possibilities. *This is about getting it right.* Accordingly, courage is a virtue, the midpoint between cowardice and heedlessness. Prudence is a virtue between the extremes of hedonism and complete self-denial. Aristotle established a code of ethics around the intellectual and moral virtues, all of which relied on free will and a sense of civic obligation. Conservatives would be quite at home with most, if not all, of it. Key here is that Aristotle maintained that these virtues were identifiable points, they weren't relative or changing, and they were somewhere near the middle of prevailing thought—not advancing outward toward a new extreme as progress demands. Thus, in important ways, conservatism was both realistic (promoting moderation or midpoints) and idealistic (that humans could organize political life around such concepts).

A nuanced appreciation for Aristotle and for the unique political culture we forged at the founding is essential for conservatives
today. As is clear from this book, my political views were heavily
influenced by Ronald Reagan. Reagan inspired us with the "shin-
ing city on a hill" metaphor of American life. This invokes John
Winthrop and the Puritans who set sail for America in the early
seventeenth century with the mission of establishing a faith-based
society that would be an example for all people, for all time. That
was summoning then, and it continues to be so today. Likewise,
Locke, Smith, and other Enlightenment thinkers influenced our
Founders and inspired us to be bold, establishing a form of government based on the individual and natural rights from God.
However, we should not fall in to the trap of uncritical, unqualified Enlightenment thought. There are limits to progress, namely
that there are universal truths and that there is a difference
between right and wrong.

Our unique political culture attenuated the influence of the
Enlightenment with the contributions of Rousseau. If we look
closely, we will see Rousseau on the road to Paris in 1749, cautioning
us about the dangers of the Parisian salon, and asking us to remember that life can't simply be reduced to equations, science, and "progress." We have a soul and we have free will. We are responsible for
our lives and we must make choices. Sometimes that may mean
sacrifice for the good of family members, friends, and others in the
community.

We are Lockean—we believe in a capitalistic, free enterprise
system, but we temper that with a Judeo-Christian code of conduct
that instructs us to remember that at the end of the day, we are
striving to live a life in step with virtue. That blending of Locke and
Rousseau, progress and virtue, worldly success and Jesus-inspired
selflessness—our political culture is truly unique—represents one

of the greatest gifts the American experiment has given to mankind. Thus it is important to remember that faith is also important to conservatives from a civic perspective. We must keep faith with founding principles.

Close examination of our founding documents evidences genius and Aristotelian balance. While we established a government with virtue in the system—"ambition to counteract ambition" and countervailing forces to preserve liberty (the separation of powers, federalism, and the Bill of Rights)—in our politics, we never stop looking for the virtuous man or woman to lead us. We enacted a Constitution that provides for enduring truths and virtues, but we allowed it to evolve over time in a way that made constitutional change possible, but especially difficult. Think about it: At once we have the longest-standing stable constitution in the world right now, and we've only amended it twenty-seven times. The point here is that the Founders did their best to put a stake in the ground regarding what they thought "right" and "wrong" looked like. Yet they also had the wisdom to accept the reality that new truths would be discovered over time, and therefore it was important to allow for a process of change, but that any proposed changes had to meet an especially high threshold before enactment. It was genius, and it has worked.

The Meaning of Plymouth Rock

Today, progressives and conservatives fight over the original intent of the Founders regarding the separation of church and state. Pointing to the First Amendment that prohibits the Congress from establishing a state religion, progressives claim we are a secular state where faith should not be invoked in the realm of civic duty. This is a wrong reading of original intent, and conservatives need to push back and engage spiritedly in this debate. Much weighs in the balance.

Based on bad experience in England, early settlers emigrated to America to worship as they were called. Religious liberty played an instrumental role in the establishment of our country. Life in early America was very difficult and dangerous. Settlers took great risk to live free, to worship God in accordance with their beliefs. For the first century and a half of our existence, the English crown continued to pressure colonists to comply with the state-established Anglican Church. Colonists resisted, and after winning independence, the Founders protected religious liberty by enshrining it with the First Amendment. Henceforth in this new nation, citizens were free to live out their faith.

That rock-solid commitment to religious liberty should not be confused with secularism. The Founders never intended to keep God out of civic and government life. Everywhere one looks, you can find evidence of that. God figures prominently in our social contract, the Declaration of Independence. Indeed, we acknowledge our Creator and credit Him with providing us natural rights, among them life, liberty, and the promise of a flourishing life, where we can rise to our potential. The Declaration of Independence is then the predicate for the Constitution, which acknowledges the Creator in the ratification clause, "in the Year of our Lord one thousand seven hundred and Eighty seven." Moreover, dating back to the opening session of the Continental Congress in 1774, our national legislature began session in prayer. Nearly all of the signers of the Constitution were leaders in their local churches, many the head of focused Bible studies. Further, the correspondence of these leaders is replete with references to God. There can be no doubt that we were founded to be, as our modern Pledge of Allegiance states, "one nation, under God, indivisible, with liberty and justice for all." The United States has never been a secular state.

At the same time, conservatives must remember that we were firmly established with the principle of religious liberty, and while that was in the Judeo-Christian tradition, our Constitution protects all faiths. That founding document prohibits religious tests. As we grapple with security issues in a post-9/11 world, we must not lose sight of who we are—all religions, including Islam, are welcome in America, where we are a nation of laws, strengthened by faith. Finally, it is important for all Americans to recognize how vital faith is to our republic. Without it, we will not be able to revitalize our republic and strengthen the American dream. The foundation of this great experiment in self-governance rested on faith—in God, ourselves, our family and friends, and this exceptional way of life.

Faith and the American Dream

In his first inaugural address, President Reagan shared with the nation the story of an obscure young barber from Cherokee, Iowa, named Martin Treptow who enlisted in the National Guard to fight for our nation during World War I. Serving with the 42nd "Rainbow" Division during the Second Battle of the Marne in July 1918, Private Treptow lost his life while volunteering to carry a message to another unit during a pivotal moment in the fight. On his body, they found a diary with the following passage:

America must win this war. I will work, I will save, I will sacrifice, I will endure, I will fight cheerfully and do my utmost, as if the issue of the whole struggle depended on me alone.

Treptow embodied the spirit of the American citizen, always keeping faith with our cherished way of life. As we serve God and our fellow man, we must keep faith in ourselves and our ability to be self-governing. Unlike under divine right of kings, when the crown provided security and government, in our republic sovereignty and security count on *us*. Our God-given right to a flourishing life counts on us to establish a government, participate in it to ensure viability and justice, and provide for the common defense of our liberties. Our republic counts on the citizen to help shape the law, and thereafter follow it. Our government draws its legitimacy from the consent of the governed. Although the first responsibility of government is to protect its people and their liberty, the Founders envisioned the citizen playing an instrumental role in national security by being personally armed and trained in a local militia.

As citizens with free will, when we conducted ourselves in a virtuous and honorable way, we not only enhanced life in the republic, we also secured salvation as our eternal reward in the afterlife. All of this is predicated on humans keeping faith in themselves—that we would be able to fulfill all of these duties and responsibilities. Life as a citizen is clearly much more demanding than life as a subject of the crown. The Founders recognized these realities and did what they could to help prepare citizens for them, both with their personal example and in their writings. Ben Franklin, for example, published several works that attempted to illuminate, including *The Autobiography of Benjamin Franklin*. Citizens were required to take personal responsibility for their lives and be prepared to do hard things.

Much of our early political thought on conduct was dominated by the writings of Aristotle and his theories on virtue and character. Leadership by example was essential, as virtue was

largely taught by a mentor who exhibited strong moral character and helped instill morality in the young American through
constant feedback and daily habit. Parenting was a high priority
in American life. Of course, given the structure of the economy
back then, it was easier to accomplish these tasks. Agriculture was
the primary driver, and it was not uncommon to have three generations living together on the farm. Thus young ones had the
benefit of both parents and grandparents as they found their way
in the world.

Today, extended families living together is very rare. Over the
years, the family structure has changed. First, with the onset of
the industrial age, we saw mass migration to cities and the family
composition evolving from extended to nuclear structure. With
the transformation from industrial to information age economies,
the family unit has seen further disintegration, with single-parent
homes now common. The breakdown of the family has caused
significant social upheaval and marked alienation, especially
among children of divorced couples. The result is undeniable—
more citizens lacking confidence in their personal and professional lives, which has translated into, among other things, lower
levels of civic participation. Voting rates among the young are
down, and Millennials are increasingly disenchanted with both
political parties. We are losing faith in our ability to live up to the
responsibilities of citizenship.

Our country has faced significant challenges in the past.
What is different this time is that for the first time, we lack confidence in ourselves—that we can solve our problems. In part,
this lack of confidence in ourselves and our elected leaders carried Donald Trump to the presidency. Some early polling in the
2016 presidential campaign illustrated that point. Among all the
shared characteristics of early Trump supporters was belief in

authoritarianism. Authoritarianism refers to the preference for antidemocratic approaches in which one person is given extraordinary powers to solve vexing political problems. For those who covet liberty, this development was particularly concerning. In some ways, this is German idealism taken to an extreme with Trump as Nietzsche's "*Übermensch*" exercising "will to power." As evidenced by this election, when Americans become increasingly frustrated with the political process, they are more open to supporting a "strong man" who can deliver us from the seemingly intractable problems of economic decline, political divisiveness, and gridlock.

If our republic is to survive, we must overcome this crisis of confidence. We must keep faith in ourselves, and in our family and friends, that we are still capable of being a self-governing people. To unify our nation and overcome difficult circumstances, we must rediscover citizenship, not continue the trend of centralizing power in the executive branch. Inspiring citizens through more civic education and a focus on American history will help. Having civic leaders who emphasize the important role of citizens in this republic will also contribute. Toward that end, leadership by example will be paramount. As citizens, we also need to help and encourage each other to do our part. That means positive reinforcement when we are meeting or exceeding expectations and being held accountable when we do not, including shaming behavior when it is detrimental to the community.

Shame and Redemption

A healthy republic begins with productive and engaged citizens and supportive families and communities. Strong families help raise and support young citizens. Parents play an instrumental role in modeling good behavior and cultivating happy, healthy, productive, contributing members of society. Supporting marriage is central to that effort.

I married my first wife shortly after turning twenty-three years old. I had high hopes and dreams, but ultimately the marriage did not last. We divorced six years later without children. Although society did not foist this upon me, I felt shame. It was an appropriate emotion. In the Catholic Church, divorce is certainly looked down upon. Marriage is both a sacrament and a responsibility, as the family unit plays a pivotal role in a free society. Marriages fail for a variety of reasons. Both parties play a role, and for me it was no different. As a young military officer, I did not live life in balance. I put too much priority on work, and my marriage suffered as a result.

Shame plays a constructive role for society. When we are selfish, unfairly treating others, or letting society down due to lack of effort, shame motivates us to change, to live up to our obligations to others. Shame is not meant to be a permanent disposition. Rather, it is intended to be a catalyst for an introspective process that ideally ends in personal improvement and redemption.

That was my experience. My divorce led to a period of painful introspection and, with the help of the Catholic Church, personal growth and ultimately redemption. The annulment process required me to provide extensive testimony and participate in priest-led counseling. A mirror was put up to my life, and all of that led to important insights and recommitment to a life following Christ, and the possibility for the sacrament of marriage once again in the church. I am deeply grateful for God's mercy. I am now in a different place emotionally and psychologically, prepared to fully meet my responsibilities as a husband and father. This process of shame, recognition of failure, contrition, and recommitment to excellence has provided me with the opportunity of redemption and a flourishing life in all aspects.

Mary Jo and I were married with a papal blessing in October 1996, and we have been happily married for over twenty-one years now. We have three wonderful children who are beginning their own journeys in faith. My ex-wife, too, has found redemption, a new marriage, and children of her own. While I wouldn't wish the painful experience of divorce on anyone, I am deeply grateful for the opportunity of redemption.

Gibson family photo at home in 2014. Left to right: Connor, Mary Jo, me, Maggie, and Katie.

America has often been described as the "land of second chances." We hear stories of that every day. Redemption plays an essential role in that process. Listening to Tim McGraw explain it, it was clear that Tug McGraw's life was fuller once he embraced his son. As humans, we are not perfect. Our exceptional American way of life is built upon some critical assumptions—that we will work hard, commit ourselves to excellence, and play well with others. Our unique political culture certainly counts on that. We have a Lockean-based economic system—capitalism—where we are judged based on our merits, achievements, and failures. That way of life, decidedly competitive, has produced the most freedom and prosperity for mankind in the history of the world. We shouldn't change it. However, in our political culture we balance capitalism with a strong commitment to family and community to support one another in our personal lives. That balanced approach also helps provide meaning in our lives. When we personally fail on either of these responsibilities, we must take responsibility. Shame from our fellow citizens helps play a constructive role bringing that in focus, but shame should only be a temporary state en route to a reconstructed, productive, and happy condition, where we once again thrive and flourish in step with excellence and virtue.

We all can take inspiration from the redemptive life of Paul of the New Testament. Before he was Paul, he was Saul, a murderer of Christians. Saul's behavior was evil and his life seemed beyond hope. Yet on his way to Damascus, he was literally "blinded by the light," and accepted Jesus as his savior. His life completely changed and he was redeemed. He helped spread the gospel and brought hope to many. If someone like Saul can be redeemed, then we too can receive forgiveness for our sins and live a reconstructed, flourishing life.

A flourishing life is not a destination point, it is a journey, and we are all striving for self-improvement. Each day we rise, we endeavor to be better than the last. When we are at our best, this ethos defines American life. By strengthening our commitment to this dialectic process and applying it to all facets of our personal and professional lives, we will tackle hard problems and regain confidence. That will be essential to revitalizing our republic and strengthening the American dream.

Hassan

Our founding principles and values have played an instrumental role in our nation's success to date. We have always kept faith in the citizen—that we could govern and secure ourselves. We are different from Europe, and the rest of the world, by choice. We must remember that, especially during the challenging and stressful times. When faced with economic dislocation, political divide, and international challenge, the answer is not to discard founding principles and empower a "strong man" to deliver us from peril.

The choices Americans faced in the 2016 presidential race were horrific. I voted for Donald Trump because I could not accept the alternative, but I am concerned about where this is headed. Our Founders decided to limit and separate governmental powers to prevent tyrannical abuse that would threaten liberty. Not content with the limits on national institutions, they established auxiliary checks, empowering states and codifying a Bill of Rights. Our Founders chose liberty over efficiency. They were well aware that centralizing power in a single person with executive authority would make political change easier and faster, but they consciously decided against that. The political "strong man" is not the answer to our problems—it's the problem. Rather than centralizing and consolidating powers, we should instead rededicate ourselves to restoring founding principles, keeping faith with our exceptional way of life. As the Trump administration proceeds, we must all keep this in mind.

President Trump's campaign pledge to bring back torture was particularly concerning. Torture defiles human life and is inconsistent with a republican form of government established to elevate the individual. Torture not only violates our values, it also doesn't work, because information gained from it is not reliable.

During a deployment to Mosul, Iraq, my battalion achieved battlefield success in part due to valuable intelligence gained from a detainee who was surprised by the kind treatment he received from U.S. forces. His name was Hassan and he was a machine gunner with the local insurgent group—we called them the "Santa Fe Gang," after the road given the same name by coalition forces in northwest Mosul. We badly wounded and captured Hassan during a big gunfight with this determined enemy during the first week of January 2005. He was evacuated to the nearby MASH unit, where he was treated for his wounds and began to heal.

When Command Sergeant Major Richard Flowers and I interrogated him a couple of days later, he was in disbelief. For quite a while, he could not fathom why we were helping him. He figured there had to be a nefarious reason why he had received medical treatment that saved his life. He expected to be executed. We explained that as Americans, we follow the Geneva Convention and the Law of Land Warfare, which dictated that he receive treatment once he was a noncombatant.

Evidently impressed by that conduct, Hassan began to affiliate with us over the course of the next several days. In the process, he shared the locations and identities of the entire Santa Fe Gang. After verifying that information with other human and technical collection resources available to us, we prepared for a nighttime raid to kill or capture these insurgents. The preparation for this operation took close to a week. There was extensive planning, coordination, and rehearsal—this would be a high-risk operation. We were targeting about twenty known insurgents. As the date for the operation drew near, our affiliation with Hassan got stronger. We learned of his family concerns and offered to help with them after the operation. Then we asked if he would be willing to accompany us on the raid to ensure we went to the right houses where the insurgents lived. He agreed to do that for us. This resulted in a highly successful operation. We captured sixteen insurgents without firing a shot. The element of surprise and the coordinated nature of the operation (we simultaneously entered all the houses) made that so.

The next day, Command Sergeant Major Flowers and I walked the streets of that neighborhood to hear directly from those who lived there, their reaction to our operation. We walked the entire block, interacting with dozens of Iraqis on the street. We were prepared for anything. To our delight, the community seemed relieved that those insurgents had been captured and removed from the area, even some of their own family members. One of the nephews of an insurgent came up to me and said, "You took away my uncle!" To which I responded, "He was conducting violent attacks and had to be detained." The boy responded, "Okay, can I have a soccer ball?" This was initially confusing, but I quickly realized the boy was satisfied with my response and was taking advantage of our encounter to ask for a soccer ball, which Iraqi children knew commanders often traveled with to pass out to neighborhoods that followed security rules. I gave him that ball. Flowers, from Brooklyn, was incredulous. "Sir, you take that guy's uncle and he asks for a soccer ball. You wouldn't see that in the projects." Flowers always had a way of injecting humor into serious situations.

That successful raid essentially defeated the Santa Fe Gang. We were able to further strengthen the security environment over the next ten days, and subsequently the election went off without incident. This was welcome news for our higher headquarters, which only weeks earlier had taken a bleak outlook on that possibility. Hassan proved instrumental in that success. Before that nighttime raid, we were making contact on an almost daily basis with the Santa Fe Gang; after it, we had virtually no contact. Affiliating with Hassan made all the difference, and when we processed his detainee packet for Iraqi justices, we recorded that cooperation and his prison sentence reflected that assistance. American values, not torture, helped produced that success. We must keep faith in our values; they have been instrumental to the success of our nation.

Out of the Darkness

Life is hard, but there can be nobility in the struggle when we live committed to virtue. We are here to support one another in this journey. As Tocqueville documented, among the greatest strengths in our country has always been the volunteer and not-for-profit organizations within our communities. They make a huge positive difference. This simply would not be so without our extraordinary volunteers. My wife, Mary Jo, is one of them. I have been awed by her work. She is a licensed clinical social worker (LCSW) who works part-time in the behavioral health clinic at the local VA helping veterans with PTSD, and she volunteers across the community, including leading efforts to combat suicide, lifting awareness and prevention. Mary Jo took me to "Out of the Darkness" walks throughout our district to promote awareness and education, support families who have lost loved ones to suicide, and help those in mental health crisis.

These walks were very powerful events filled with mixed and heavy emotions. Many of the attendees are family and friends coping with a recent loss. Others are mental health professionals or media personalities who are helping to provide focus and resources for this scourge. We hear testimonials, often heartwrenching, sometimes uplifting, but always emotionally charged. At one of these walks, intervention was arranged for an individual who came with suicidal ideations. More than anything, the walks were a real opportunity to bond and provide mutual support. We have made deep friendships through this cause. I always come away from them drained, but also heartened that as Americans we support each other in time of crisis and need. It is important that we sustain these organizations so essential to helping us keep faith. Federal and state governments can help with financial support for suicide awareness and prevention and resources for mental health, but the real work is done in our communities. The human connection is vital.

Mary Jo brought this message to Washington, D.C., where she was one of the founding cochairs of the Congressional Spouses Group for suicide prevention, which is partnered with the American Foundation for Suicide Prevention. These spouses promote mental health support activities, including the aforementioned "Out of the Darkness" walks across the nation. They are making a positive difference, helping people keep faith and gain access to resources and support to help them through challenging times.

As Americans, we have busy lives with competing priorities. Through it all we experience many successes and failures. Sometimes we walk in the darkness. It is important to keep perspective and keep faith as we move toward the light. We must also keep faith in our exceptional way of life—that balance between promoting upward mobility and freedom for the individual and fulfilling our commitments to family, friends, and community. That is the best way to walk out of the darkness. I have done my best to lead by example on that score. Life's journey has taught me that by far my most important responsibilities are as husband and father.

Speaking at the "Out of the Darkness" walk for suicide awareness and prevention on the Walkway over the Hudson bridge that connects Ulster and Dutchess Counties in New York.

From the very beginning, this nation was founded upon faith, protecting religious liberty. These religious covenants inform our obligations to each other in both our private and public lives. The strength of our nation starts with responsible citizens and strong families who cherish their freedom and honor their commitments to others. As we seek to revitalize our republic and strengthen the American dream, it is paramount that we keep faith—in God, ourselves, our family and friends, our community, and this exceptional nation.

CHAPTER 5

Unify and Grow

Winning!

A few days before the 2014 midterm election, the *New York Times* ran a story with the headline "G.O.P. Representative in Upstate New York Is Strong among Democrats."

Considering the source, it might as well have read "Man Bites Dog." The political writer, Michael Barbaro, started the story with:

> A local Democratic lawmaker is casting a vote on Tuesday for Representative Chris Gibson, a Republican, "because he's down to earth." A longtime volunteer for Democratic campaigns is supporting Mr. Gibson "because he's run a positive campaign." A retired Democratic union worker will back Mr. Gibson because, after an hour-long meeting, he concluded that "Chris is a good man."

Barbaro went on to add he found the congressional race "rare" and "intriguing" because it was "a case study of how a Republican can cultivate, win over and retain an unusually high level of support from Democrats in a swing district, while adhering to Republican positions."

Republican congressional leaders in Washington, D.C., were stunned by this story and the election outcome that followed—my margin of victory was 65 percent to 35 percent. National Republican Congressional Committee (NRCC) chairman Representative Greg Walden, knowing that I had been outspent by my Democratic opponent in that campaign by two to one, in a congressional district that President Barack Obama carried by more than six points in 2012, wondered out loud how this was possible. In the paragraphs that follow, I explain. The story of how we earned such strong support across the ideological spectrum, from hardcore Tea Party followers to committed liberals, can serve as a blueprint for the conservative movement as we seek to unify and grow our ranks in the coming years.

Just "Chris"

My political career started on March 6, 2010, just six days after I had retired from the U.S. Army. Our family made the decision to retire from the Army to answer the calling of national leadership— to help our country come together and move forward. To do so, I came directly from brigade command in the 82nd Airborne Division, a stepping-stone to the general officer ranks. It was never about what rank I achieved anyway. It was always about the service, and now I was getting a change of mission.

The summer of 2009 was a rough one for the country. After passage of a near $1 trillion stimulus package and consideration of a government-dominated health care proposal (later known as Obamacare), a political awakening occurred throughout the nation, spawning the Tea Party movement and very acrimonious town hall meetings across America. Politically, the country was coming apart, and I felt I had something valuable to add, helping our country unite to address national problems.

This wasn't a decision my family made lightly. I've studied history extensively and taught American politics at West Point—I knew that the transition from senior military officer to elected leader was not always easy and successful. Some, like Senator John McCain, a former Navy captain, succeeded, while others, like Generals Wesley Clark and Pete Dawkins, failed, despite very impressive service records of demonstrated leadership. Clark culminated his career as a four-star general officer commanding all forces in Europe. Dawkins was a veritable Army icon—a Heisman Trophy winner, All-American halfback while on the West Point football team who went on to be a Rhodes Scholar, distinguished infantry officer decorated for valor in Vietnam, and the first person in his class to make general officer. These two soldiers were the epitome of success in the Army, but both failed when running for elected office. As I considered running for office myself, I studied a number of cases like these. I learned that many of the skills, traits, and characteristics of successful senior military officers were also desirable for effective elected leaders, such as developing shared vision, communicating, managing, and leading.

The biggest difference between the two is that for the military, the hierarchical command structure requires subordinates to follow orders. In politics, people have a choice. Although former senior military leaders are well suited to make that transition, some are uncomfortable not being crisply saluted after giving instructions. After more than thirty years of internalizing the hierarchical system, some view themselves as the rank they hold, and when they become first-time political candidates, that can turn off voters. Former senior military leaders have to be comfortable with voters calling them by their first name. If they bristle or grimace, voters pick up on the presumption and the opportunity for connection is lost. Politics is an intensely personal business and Americans are fiercely proud of traditions where aspiring political leaders humble themselves and *ask* for support.

These thoughts were on my mind as I was making the transition. In February 2010, I was an Army colonel—a brigade commander in the 82nd Airborne Division with command responsibility for more than forty-five hundred men and women. In March, however, I knew it would be just "Chris" attempting to earn the support of my fellow citizens, aspiring to serve them as their representative in Congress. I would be "interviewing" with more than seven hundred thousand people for this job, and each and every one of them would be my boss if I won.

In the first week of March, more than 150 family and friends gathered at the local country club in my hometown of Kinderhook to welcome me home and to launch our congressional campaign. It was a very special event, replete with guest speakers and a slide show of old childhood photos and images from throughout my twenty-nine years in the military. Onstage, I had an emotional moment myself mentioning my dad, wishing he could be with us for this wonderful occasion. Dad had passed away in 2008. Standing up on that stage was very exciting, but it was also deeply humbling. In the Army, I knew my soldiers were counting on me to get it right so that we accomplished the mission while keeping them safe. Now I was aspiring to be a representative, and that came with enormous responsibility too. I had to learn all facets of public policy and where my people were on the issues of the day. I was ever conscious of that—I did not want to disappoint. When the event finally ended, I was drained. It was certainly a success, as we raised a decent amount of money and received significant media coverage, but I also knew this was the beginning of a long and difficult road.

Quite frankly, in those early days no serious political observer thought we could win. The NRCC, fully committed to dozens of other more competitive races across the country, was not impressed with my chances and told me so the following month during a visit to Washington. Local GOP leaders encouraged me, but they too knew this was going to be a significant uphill struggle. The incumbent, Representative Scott Murphy, a Democrat, had won a special election the previous year after Kirsten Gillibrand was elevated from that seat to the U.S. Senate. Gillibrand had won her reelection to our House seat in 2008 with 62 percent of the vote, and Murphy appeared off to a strong start, popular among voters, and had over $1 million in his campaign account. We, on the other hand, had no name recognition, no money, and no national support.

I remained optimistic throughout. I was certain we would not be outworked. Even though I am a lifelong New York Jets fan (it generally comes as a package deal when one is a New York Mets fan), I've always been inspired by legendary Green Bay Packers coach Vince Lombardi's philosophical approach to life. Lombardi often stated that while the "will to win" was important, it was not as important as the "will to *prepare* to win." Simply put— *hard work matters.*

From the Army, I brought with me an organizational approach that empowered people. There were ten counties in the 20th Congressional District of New York, and we needed to have focused grassroots organizing, outreach, fund-raising, and media efforts in each of them. Picking the right person to lead these efforts in each county was essential. Fortunately, I had help from seasoned hands—Steve Bulger of Saratoga County, Rich Crist of Rensselaer County, and Mark Westcott of Warren County had over fifty years of experience between them leading winning campaigns. They also led by example, serving as "Team Gibson" county coordinators for their respective areas. I counted on them to help me gain situational awareness, build relationships with community leaders, understand local issues, ensure I attended important community events, help us raise money, and connect me with voters in their area—including organizing "meet and greets" and rallies where media was present. Using this methodical approach, working fourteen- to sixteen-hour days, and posting frequently on Facebook, we quickly gained the reputation of being *everywhere* in the district.

These activities impressed NRCC leadership, but overall they were still skeptical. I was behind on fund-raising goals, given my late start getting home from the Army. The election was less than seven months away and I had very little cash on hand in our campaign account. They also were alarmed by some of our campaign priorities, like early use of "Gibson for Congress" lawn signs. "Lawn signs don't win elections," I was told. Of course, I knew that, but this was a conscious choice to help raise awareness of our campaign. Half of our counties had no restrictions on when lawn signs could be put up, so we asked our supporters to emplace them as early as April.

Very quickly we had hundreds of simple, catchy, easily read "Gibson for Congress" signs on lawns across those counties. Studies show that humans generally need at least three exposures before they retain an image in long-term memory, and we kept that in mind when placing signs. We received good feedback on this tactic. For example, when I attended a barbecue in rural Washington County in June, as I introduced myself to the attendees, who numbered over two hundred, I asked if they had heard of me. Most said no. Then I showed them a piece of my campaign literature with the Gibson lawn sign, and that prompted a quick response. "Oh, you're the sign guy—I've seen your signs—you have a lot of support!"

Later in the campaign when our first TV commercial was aired district-wide, we consciously made the last image of the advertisement the "Gibson for Congress" lawn sign. We wanted folks to make the connection—this was a commercial from that Army veteran who had all that personal support among the grass roots. The commercial worked as intended. Our supporters were getting questions from their neighbors: "I saw Gibson's commercial. He was in the military and fought for our country. I noticed you have his sign—have you met him? What's he like?"

Supporters put out "Gibson for Congress" lawn signs across the district to help build name recognition.

More than anything, the major takeaway was that people matter. To be competitive, a candidate needs to raise the requisite amount of money to be on TV, radio, the digital space, and in print (mail and newspaper advertisements), but at the end of the day, what moves votes more than anything is the personal endorsement of men and women of character. When your strong supporters vouch for you with their family, friends, and coworkers at their volunteer organizations (the Elks Lodge, American Legion, firehouse, and so on), and with neighbors while at the store or at their kids' baseball, softball, and soccer games, poll numbers begin to move and your campaign gains momentum.

My approach to campaign fund-raising was also unconventional, which did not engender early confidence at the NRCC. Congressional candidates are expected to spend many hours a day "dialing for dollars," cold-calling prospective donors asking for money for the campaign. I did this for a day. I called for about eight hours and got two people on the line—for the rest, I left voicemail messages. I talked about that unsatisfying experience with Mary Jo at dinner and thought about it late into the evening, struggling with what to do. I was new to politics, but my gut told me that approach would not work. Ultimately I decided to go in another direction. When I reported for work the next day and saw my consultant, he said, "Are you ready for another day of calls?" "No," I proclaimed. He said, "Then you really don't want to be a congressman." I then asked him, "If I called you out of the blue and asked you to give me money, would you write me a check?" He didn't respond. *Exactly*, I thought.

Still, we needed an effective plan to raise a lot of money, and we needed it yesterday. I directed our team to make a list of all the prospective donors, those people who might be inclined to support our campaign (essentially that same list of people I was supposed to cold-call). I then asked, "Who among our early supporters personally knows these prospective donors?" Then, rather than my leaving a voicemail with the prospective donor, we asked our advocates to contact the targets to arrange a time for me to personally meet with them. The key point was that our advocate and the prospective donor already had a relationship. There was a better chance they would take a call from their friend or associate than from me, someone they didn't know. Once the personal meeting was arranged, it was my responsibility to win over the donor, to get them to join our cause.

This indirect approach required much more effort than just cold-calling, but in the end it proved more effective. Instead of dialing for dollars, I spent a lot of time traveling across the district to diners, country clubs, restaurants, and homes for high-stakes one-on-one sessions. This increased fund-raising productivity and voter contact across the district. After we inspired some of these donors to join our cause, they introduced me to their friends and associates, who also contributed. Many of these people, influential in their communities, also put up "Gibson for Congress" lawn signs, and that public endorsement also helped build momentum for our cause. The bottom line: We raised $1.65 million in the last seven months of the campaign and met thousands of voters before election day.

It was at the smaller gatherings with voters I found I was at my best—connecting with people on an emotional level and hearing directly the kind of representation they desired in Washington. Quickly we started amassing a sizable list of volunteers committed to going door-to-door, making phone calls, and conducting "sign waves" across the district to demonstrate enthusiasm and raise name recognition. By the early fall we had over four thousand volunteers, and I mentioned to the team that that was about the size of my brigade in the 82nd Airborne. Some of the volunteers got a kick out of this and started calling themselves the "Gibson Brigade." I was fine with whatever they named themselves, because they were remarkably effective at bringing our message across the district. It was also a lot of fun. Mary Jo and I found we really enjoyed this new experience, cherishing the time we spent with our volunteers—friendships we've kept to this day.

By early September, some polling began to show signs of our competitiveness, and the NRCC finally put me in their "Young Guns" program. That status has to be earned, but once thresholds are reached regarding popular support, campaign organization, and fund-raising goals, national resources begin to flow. We were deeply grateful—candidly, we needed the help. I was being significantly outspent at that point. Commercials for Congressman Murphy went on the air in mid-August, a full month before I could afford to do so. With the NRCC now all in, our confidence was lifted.

In upstate New York, independent polling from the Siena Research Institute carries a lot of weight, especially among the media, and when their results came in mid-September, it slowed our momentum. According to their survey, we were down seventeen points with just six weeks to go. I had spent the last several weeks unsuccessfully trying to get more TV coverage for our campaign, seeking stories that would cover my position on a particular issue or highlight our participation in an important local event. Reporters weren't interested in these "good news" stories. Once the results of the poll came out, however, we didn't even have to call media outlets—TV cameras were waiting for me at the Clifton Park campaign office that afternoon. Reporters queued up to ask me challenging questions: "Does this mean your message is failing with voters?" "Maybe you are wrong and the voters like Obamacare—your reaction to that?" "Murphy appears more likable among the voters; do you agree?" My response to all of them was that I needed to work harder. The voters were just getting to know me and I remained optimistic that once we reached them we would win. I felt good about how I handled that unpleasant experience, but it didn't immediately translate. After those interviews, all of the media coverage dwelled on my significant deficit in the polls. Analysts deemed I was in trouble and that my campaign was faltering. Then came the debates.

Maggie Saves the Race!

Probably the most memorable moment of that first campaign came during our debate at Queensbury High School in early October when I landed a decisive blow on my opponent after he claimed I was shipping jobs overseas. He had no idea I was lying in ambush for that ridiculous claim, and he couldn't have known that the author of my effective retort was probably the most shocking of sources—our eleven-year-old daughter, Maggie.

The epiphany occurred a couple nights earlier as our family was driving to a gathering of friends on Kinderhook Lake. Just before we arrived, one of Scott Murphy's attack advertisements played on the radio. I was hoping somehow that no one was paying attention. It was quite embarrassing to be in the presence of my entire family, including our preteen children, and hearing a commercial kicking my teeth in. The narrator claimed I was shipping jobs overseas and otherwise causing the utter destruction of civilization as we know it. Any hope that this broadside against my character went over the heads of my loved ones was dashed when Maggie's voice rose up from the backseat of our red Chrysler Town & Country minivan. She said, "Dad, the only thing you've shipped overseas was your paratroopers. What is this guy talking about?" Immediately a light bulb went off inside my head. I turned to Mary Jo and said, "That was pretty good." "Yeah, I agree," she replied. The next night, in our last debate preparation meeting, when that question came up, I shared with the team not to worry. I had a zinger prepared.

Then came the moment. The Queensbury crowd was definitely

into the debate—both sides were animated and boisterous throughout. Just before closing remarks, Murphy, as if on cue, went on a diatribe, claiming I shipped jobs overseas. When it was my turn, I started giving a thoughtful policy-oriented response on how best to create jobs and facilitate rising wages for workers. It looked like your typical Republican response. Then, as I closed, I turned directly to Murphy, paused for dramatic effect, and let it rip: "And Scott, for the record, the only thing I've shipped overseas in the last decade was me and my paratroopers, to fight for *your* freedom!" Then I stared him down for a few more seconds as the Queensbury crowd, close to a thousand strong, leapt to their feet in a thunderous roar. Murphy looked absolutely crestfallen. He was a beaten man.

The 11:00 p.m. TV news cycle covered that segment of the debate, making mention of the crowd's highly supportive reaction. The good media coverage extended into the next day, and I was subsequently asked about it at every campaign stop over the next several days, giving further legs to the story. By week's end it was clear that the momentum of the campaign had changed. We now had a noticeable edge. This continued for the next two weeks until the final Siena Research Institute poll was released eight days before the election. The results were stark—there had been a twenty-six-point shift and I was now leading by nine points! What an amazing turnaround in just five weeks.

We went on to win 55 percent to 45 percent on election night—a decisive victory. It was driven by grassroots organization and support. Our volunteers made all the difference. We ran an unconventional campaign that emphasized the strength of ordinary people, reflected in the power-down approach organized around county coordinators. I had no big-name consultants and a local pollster, Patrick Lanne, who turned out to be one of the best in the business. We had close to a thousand supporters packed into the

Saratoga Springs Holiday Inn banquet room for the victory celebration. It was a night I will never forget, and as I took to the stage for my remarks, I looked over at Maggie and thought, "If people only knew who won our battle of Gettysburg—who helped craft the counterattack line that took down Scott Murphy—they wouldn't believe it."

Now you know *the rest of the story.*

Our volunteers would often stage "sign waves" to raise name recognition and demonstrate momentum.

Trust

After that upset victory, I was sworn in during the first week of January 2011 and went on to serve six years in the U.S. House of Representatives. Ultimately I retired from Congress undefeated and unindicted. That used to mean nothing in politics, but sadly, these days that low bar is an accomplishment in itself. As you can see from the previous section, winning a congressional race the first time presents certain challenges. To be *reelected*, you have to be able to demonstrate that you did what you pledged you would do during the initial campaign. You must earn and keep trust. You must also have thick skin, constantly showing a desire to improve, demonstrating the ability to learn from mistakes.

Part of getting better means examining closely what goes right and wrong with a campaign. Following an election, it is common practice for both parties to conduct a postmortem—an after-action review—to understand the lessons of that campaign. Much rides on that analysis and any conclusions that follow. Sometimes we learn the wrong lessons. For example, in the aftermath of national defeat in the 2012 election, the Republican National Committee (RNC) made a mistake when they concluded that the only path back to power was to grow the party based on special interest and identity politics, such as offering amnesty to those who came here illegally. Certainly, everyone regardless of background must feel (and be) welcomed in the party, but the best way to expand support is to stand for core principles that unite the country and work for the American people. This is how we foster trust with the American people.

The 2016 presidential campaign demonstrated that a political newcomer, with no governmental experience and no fealty to the RNC, could defeat sixteen other Republican candidates in the primary, most well established in the party, and then go on to beat a Democratic dynasty in Hillary Clinton. Trump did not follow the RNC recommendations and instead attempted to forge a bond with working-class voters who've been abandoned by both political parties. I have great angst about President Trump's personal style and disagree with some of his positions that I believe are unconstitutional, but I credit him for reaching out to people like my late dad, blue-collar workers who have been collateral damage in American politics for too long. Blue-collar workers comprise every imaginable demographic—race, gender, age, sexual orientation, and so on—and deserve representation. I would not be a Republican today if it were not for Ronald Reagan's outreach to blue-collar workers, and I followed suit throughout my congressional service, proud to have the strong endorsement of the Building and Construction Trades unions.

What we need is a reconstructed and reformed Republican Party. Offering hope and solutions for workers in pursuit of upward mobility is a better strategy to win elections than relying on identity politics, which divide us from the very start. Let's keep faith in our ideas. We have the solutions to the country's pressing problems, and mounting campaigns on those principles that connect with and help the American people is the best approach to winning elections. More important, after winning on this platform, we are in a stronger position to be successful governing accordingly. This is the best way to forge and keep trust with voters.

The first step on this path is offer a clear and compelling alternative to the well-intentioned but failed "tax, borrow, and spend" statist policies of the Democratic Party. This requires rejecting the well-meaning but statist ideas of the neoconservatives within the GOP too. We already have one statist party. We don't need two.

Here's my recommendation for the reformed Republican Party platform:

1. Peace through strength. We favor a strong military as a deterrent to those who would attempt to do us harm. From a position of strength, we lead with diplomacy, commerce, and humanitarian actions. We help our friends and allies but always put America's interests first. The primary focus of our national security should be to protect Americans and our way of life, *not* regime change and nation-building around the world.

2. Liberty and founding principles. We support policies that empower citizens and help them live a flourishing life to their God-given potential. We defend the Bill of Rights—all of the first ten amendments—and the entire Constitution. We believe you don't have to give up your liberty for security. As such, we reject the Patriot Act in its current form and call for a return to our roots, that any government action impacting our rights must follow well-outlined and time-tested rules of due process of law. We stand opposed to the further consolidation of power in the executive branch and call for reform that reorders the legislative-executive branch relationship to ensure separate but equal branches of government. We reject authoritarianism and favor liberty and the messy process of self-governance in which citizens have rights and responsibilities. We believe that the free market, with all its flaws, is still the best place to facilitate prosperity and upward mobility for all of our citizens.

3. Local empowerment and home rule. We favor solutions that empower citizens and help local communities. We support states and localities as they pursue solutions to public problems. We reject the Common Core approach to education—federalizing and centralizing education policy and relying heavily on unfunded mandates and onerous high-stakes testing has not facilitated excellence. We favor instead approaches that empower students, teachers, parents, and administrators.

4. Personal responsibility. We support policies and norms that reinforce our obligations to each other in our public and private lives. We support the dignity of work and the sanctity of the family because they help us become better citizens positioned to fulfill our commitments to God and our fellow citizens. We reject bank bailouts and focus instead on holding corporate boards responsible for their action with a safety net (like FDIC) for those individual investors who may be impacted by the reckless decisions of Wall Street executives. "Too big to fail" has created moral hazard, and the Republican Party clearly shares the blame; that must change.

5. Equal opportunity and justice for all. Our party must fight for all Americans. God granted each of us natural rights, including the opportunity for a flourishing life. A quality education is essential to equal opportunity and upward mobility, and that includes emphasizing the career and technical skills so essential to promoting U.S. manufacturing and American self-reliance. We must reject crony capitalism and stop making bad trade deals. Finally, we believe that justice is blind and that no one is above or below the law. We support political reform because we believe the current political system is rigged and corrupt, and demand action to clean it up.

Some of us have been advocating positions like these for years but have been a minority voice in the party. The 2016 campaign gives me hope that the Republican Party is finally listening and connecting with the people. In my congressional district, fighting for these principles earned widespread support across the ideological spectrum and partisan divide, including among some modern-day liberals who agree with some of our classically conservative principles.

The political discourse, especially among the punditry, is sometimes confused by the distinction between conservatives and neoconservatives. For example, in 2012 the *National Journal* listed me as the "most liberal Republican" in the U.S. House because they scored as "liberal" opposing neoconservative legislation like the Patriot Act and the so-called Stop Online Piracy Act, or SOPA (new Internet regulation that would have stepped on our privacy), and because I opposed military intervention in Libya.

I campaigned on staunchly defending the Bill of Rights, fiercely advocating for liberty, and avoiding foreign entanglements that were not required to keep us safe. My constituents expected me to follow through on these conservative pledges that are consistent with founding principles. These votes and positions did just that, but they were scored as "liberal" by some media outlets and outside groups. These methodologies confuse conservative and neoconservative positions and equate "liberal" with "liberty." That is why former presidential candidate and libertarian congressman Ron Paul also ranked as the "most liberal Republican" one year and why Congressmen Justin Amash of Michigan and Tom Massie of Kentucky, noted libertarians, consistently finish near the top each year on *National Journal's* "most liberal Republican" rankings.

Out of this philosophical chaos, there is opportunity for clarity. We need clear distinction between progressive, liberal, conservative, and neoconservative approaches. Progressives favor statist approaches that empower the federal government to force equality and social justice. Neoconservatives, too, favor statist approaches (government surveillance without warrant to enhance security, federal intervention in education to improve quality, multilateral trade agreements to promote growth in the financial services and corporate sectors of the economy, bank bailouts to stabilize Wall Street meltdowns, and a militaristic foreign policy to make the world safe for democracy)—they just differ with progressives on how "big government" should be used and toward what end. Conservatives favor liberty and founding principles, which at times puts them in league with old-style liberals, which the *National Journal* acknowledges in its scorecard. Therefore, conservatives are philosophically different from progressives and neoconservatives because they reject statist approaches. Progressives and liberals have their differences, too, although in recent years they have merged, embracing statist approaches. Old-style liberals share some views with conservatives, providing possibilities for political cooperation among them in the future.

Republican leadership should recognize that although President Trump's platform wasn't philosophically coherent, his victory was clearly a repudiation of the neoconservative (sometimes called "establishment") wing of the party. Voters want a clear alternative to the statist policies of the Democratic Party. They want a liberty-minded Republican Party that seeks to maximize and defend freedom and that will fight for a flourishing life for all Americans, including the working class. Americans desire freedom, equal opportunity, upward mobility, and security—in essence, the American dream. When we focus on that we will continuously win elections with a mandate to enact our solutions. Importantly, Hispanic Americans, Black Americans, women, LGBT Americans— indeed, *Americans from all backgrounds*—will support us if we deliver on this promise. Let's stop the identity politics that divide us. Let's rally around principles that work for all of us.

Lieutenant Dan!

As a representative, my job was to give a voice in government to the nearly three-quarters of a million people in my congressional district. In my legislative work, the bills we drafted were constituent-driven, with many ideas coming directly from the people. In earlier chapters I gave examples of how we empowered farmers, providing them with an opportunity to affect farm bill legislation, and how advocates for patients suffering from chronic Lyme disease helped craft and enact legislation to combat that horrific scourge. In some of our other legislative work, we collaborated with broadband advocates to expand and improve services, veteran advocates to author legislation to improve health care, education, and housing benefits and to recognize our heroes for their service, and small business owners to draft legislation to help them grow and prosper.

I also led an effort to change my party's views on the environment. I have often said, "If conservation isn't conservative, then words have no meaning at all." We have one earth, and just as we need to manage fiscal resources to move back to a balanced budget to ensure that future generations get the same choices and freedoms we've enjoyed, likewise we must be good stewards of our natural resources to ensure that our children inherit a livable, sustainable planet. I don't support bad tax policy and onerous regulation to do that but firmly believe there are ways to promote clean and renewable energy through government-sponsored research and development and to incentivize good conservation practices through the farm bill and the Land and Water Conservation Fund. Such balanced policies help grow the economy and promote energy independence, while protecting the environment.

Championing constituent-driven legislation also helped restore faith in our ability to be self-governing. Giving a voice for my people in the legislative process made it seem that government in Washington was not that far away. At the same time, we were also laser-focused to provide the best constituent services possible for our people. From time to time constituents would call in to our office and say, "We donated to the congressman and now we need something done." Our staff would respond that while we appreciate all support, we are here to work for everyone, whether they voted for us or not, or even if they didn't vote (as much as we hoped they did). Our service was steadfast and strong for *everyone*.

Over the six years we were in office, we successfully advocated for nearly ten thousand constituents in casework that helped veterans secure the benefits and recognition they earned, that resolved problems seniors were experiencing with Social Security and Medicare, and that helped constituents applying for a passport and homeowners with mortgage problems, individuals with insurance claim disputes, and farmers and other small business owners with challenges with regulatory agencies. We also welcomed our constituents to Washington, D.C., taking them on tours of the Capitol and the White House. In short, we helped anyone in need of advocacy with the federal government.

In one particular case, we helped an Iraq War veteran get the 100 percent disability rating he was due and worked with other not-for-profit organizations to ensure that he and his family had the necessary support to deal with his life-changing injuries. Air Force technical sergeant Joe Wilkinson was an Operation Iraqi Freedom veteran, having participated in the invasion in 2003. Upon his return, Joe started experiencing weakness in his legs and other mysterious and debilitating medical problems that would ultimately confine him to a wheelchair. When we first learned of his case, his physical and mental health was declining rapidly. Joe was convinced that his deteriorating health was a direct result of exposure to highly toxic chemicals in Iraq, but he was not having success convincing the Department of Veterans Affairs of this. He and his wife reached out to our staff for help. I knew based on my experiences in Iraq that troops often came in contact with toxic chemicals. After reviewing the supporting documents Joe provided, I concluded he was right. We immediately started advocating for him. Eventually the VA relented and Joe was awarded a 100 percent service-related disability status, which entitled him to the benefits he earned as one of our nation's wounded warriors.

We were not done helping Joe and his family, however. As word of his situation spread, the community came together to help raise funds for a handicap-accessible home where Joe and his wife could raise their family. Eventually the Stephen Siller Tunnel to Towers Foundation and actor Gary Sinise agreed to help raise funds for the home. Gary Sinise is perhaps best known for his supporting role as Lieutenant Dan in the Oscar-winning movie *Forrest Gump*. He has parlayed that success into a way to help veterans through his Lt. Dan Band—a group of musicians who perform to raise money to support wounded warriors.

The Lt. Dan Band concert in Albany, New York, in 2012 helped bring together the greater Albany area for a very deserving cause. First, Sinise and I did a press event a couple of months in advance to publicize the concert. Helping focus media attention, over 250 motorcyclists rode from Joe's hometown of Nassau in Rensselaer County to the Washington Avenue Armory in Albany, where the concert was planned to take place. This helped drive attendance to the concert. When the day finally arrived, Sinise and the Lt. Dan Band put on a terrific show, electrifying the audience. It was a tremendous experience for all. The Wilkinson family was deeply grateful. That was a very special evening—one of the best during my time in Congress. In the end, I was incredibly proud of my staff for helping a wounded warrior and grateful to live in a country where neighbors come to the aid of citizens in need.

"Eighty Percent of Success Is Just Showing Up"

To be an effective representative, you have to spend a lot of time traveling the district, listening to constituents, reporting on your work, and attending important community events. It is paramount to bring your message to every corner of the district—small villages and inner cities, and every place in between. That includes going places where Republicans generally don't visit. This is important for at least two reasons. First and foremost, after the election, representatives serve everyone, regardless of whether they got their votes on election day. To properly represent, you need to listen and hear all people. Second, as former Speaker of the House Tip O'Neill used to say, if you don't ask for the vote, don't expect to get it.

My travels took me to over a thousand villages, hamlets, towns, and cities all over upstate New York. I went to soup kitchens in the inner city of Kingston, AME churches throughout the district, and charitable events far and wide. I supported causes like Habitat for Humanity, the Friends of the Upper Delaware River, land conservancies, historical societies, veterans' clubs and events, sportsmen's club events, firefighter breakfasts and dinners, farm bureau events, Little League games and events, and local chambers of commerce. I visited schools and colleges several times a month. Essentially, anytime constituents were getting together for a good cause and I had time in my schedule, I would attend.

Being a member of Congress was a seven-day-a-week job. When I wasn't in Washington in legislative session, I was out with my people. Since most community events occur over the weekend, I worked weekends. Mary Jo and our children accompanied me whenever possible, but candidly, family time was impacted by the travel demands. We knew that would be the case when I first ran for Congress, but given my self-imposed term-limit pledge, we also understood that this wouldn't be forever. To do the job right required complete family devotion to our constituents. To give a better sense of the time commitment, in 2014, counting Christmas and Easter, I had just nine days off the entire year. Certainly it was a grueling pace, but our family believed in what we were doing and drove on.

It helped that these constituent events were also the most

enjoyable aspect of the job, and when we did them as a family, it made for a strong bonding experience. Looking back on it, the whole family has tremendous memories of outings at county fairs, community days, 5K charity runs, barbecues, parades, and the like. Mary Jo and I believe that in the long run this experience should help our children to become meaningful contributors to society, and hopefully happier, too.

Without a doubt, all of these visits significantly enhanced my understanding of the district. They also ensured that I remained accessible, accountable, and transparent. Without question they also helped me gain wide support throughout the district, and that showed during election season. I found that Woody Allen was right—"eighty percent of success is just showing up."

"Party Gov"

I wrote this book during my return to academia. I'm now a professor at Williams College, but earlier in my Army career I spent three years teaching cadets at West Point. I enjoy the classroom and the opportunity to mentor America's future leaders. This has always been a priority for me, and my time in Congress was no different. Over that period I made it a priority to visit schools and colleges several times a month.

A common misperception today among some senior citizens is that civics is not taught in high school anymore. That is not true. In New York State there is a required class for high school graduation called "Participation in Government," which, as my kids informed me, is commonly referred to as "Party Gov." I was surprised by that title but frankly thankful that at least it wasn't called "PIG." Anyway, this course was often the venue for my class visits with students, although in some cases school leadership arranged for an assembly in which the entire student body participated. I generally started these sessions with an overview of my responsibilities as their representative in Congress and concluded my opening remarks with the hope that they would keep faith in our exceptional way of life. I assured them that if I could rise from a working-class family to be a colonel in the Army and later a congressman, then anything was possible in America. I also mentioned the findings of renowned sociologist Neil Howe, who has studied the generations in our country. Howe boldly asserts that "Millennials" (those born between 1982 and 2000) will rival the "Greatest Generation" in their contributions to American society. Howe explains that given the general characteristics of Millennials—that they are fiscally conservative, socially tolerant and inclusive, creative and problem solving—and the circumstances and challenges this generation faces, their collective temperament puts them in strong position to make significant reforms and tremendous positive contributions to society.

Based on my experiences in the Army, I agreed with Howe. In combat, I found our young folks to be courageous and strong. Millennials sometimes are criticized for too often playing video games and living in their parents' basements (thanks for nothing, Hillary Clinton), but my experiences were that when under fire, Millennials stepped forward. They brought the fight to the enemy. In Congress, I worked with Representative Elise Stefanik of New York, who at thirty was the youngest woman ever to be elected to Congress. As a Millennial, she is already helping shape national policy and making a positive difference. Also worth noting is that Mary Jo and I are raising three Millennials of our own. It's easy to see why Howe is so optimistic—Millennials are among the reasons why I firmly believe that as Americans, our best days are in front of us.

My school visits as a congressman reinforced these positive views.

After my opening remarks, I spent the rest of the time answering questions from students. You have to be ready for that exchange. Millennials are definitely engaged and often challenge the assumptions of previous generations. These high schoolers would ask difficult questions like: "Why is alcohol good and marijuana bad?" "Why are Republicans for a balanced budget and against the environment—isn't the point to position future generations for success?" "Why are Democrats for the environment and against a balanced budget?" "Why are Baby Boomers always fighting about everything?" One student, while framing a question like that, commented that it was as if the Vietnam War never ended. Good point.

I also visited middle schools, and occasionally elementary schools, and found that the younger the students, the more their questions focused on my military service. I learned this early on during my first term when I visited Wood Road Elementary School, part of the Ballston Spa School District. To stimulate the session, I opened up by showing a video of paratroopers jumping out of airplanes, before giving a pitch on the separation of powers and my duties as their congressman. When it came time for questions, the first student stood up and asked how I got wounded in battle. The next wanted to know what gun I carried and if I had ever fired a tank gun. After that, I was asked what it was like jumping out of an airplane. That was followed by a question about what I thought of Army food. At some point in all this I brought in the Constitution, but it was no use—young kids are naturally curious about the military, and what it's like to be a cop, firefighter, or construction worker, occupations with a heavy focus on "doing." This experience at Wood Road was not unusual; it held true across upstate New York whenever I visited elementary schools.

On the other end of the spectrum, college kids naturally asked

more nuanced, political questions. Candidly, the progressive perspective acquired from some of the faculty was also apparent. I
took no offense or alarm from that. After all, I attended graduate
school at Cornell and was used to being outnumbered and forced
to defend my conservative views. As a representative, one time I
had a constituent ask me, "What was it like being in Congress
having to debate all of those progressives?" I responded, "Are you
kidding me? I went to Cornell—at least now I'm getting paid
for it!"

I treated all of these questions, and the questioners, with respect
and candor. When I was pressed from the left, after responding, I
would often add a challenge of my own for the students: "When
professors tell you that big government is the answer, tell them
that you are open to it but want proof—show examples of when
that worked out well." Of course, there is such a thing as a public
good, and we need government to secure our liberties and a regulatory state to promote commerce, public health and safety, and
justice. The question comes down to judgment on where to draw
the line. I still believe the best way to facilitate liberty, prosperity, and upward mobility for the most number of Americans is
through the market and supporting that through volunteer organizations in our communities. We are different from the rest of
the world by choice, and that is why we have been successful promoting freedom and prosperity. The founding principles are best
for our country, and as conservatives we need to reach out to all
people, including our youth, and engage in dialogue.

I immensely enjoyed those experiences with students and
teachers. In addition to helping me be a better representative, all
of those school visits solidified my political support in the district. That helped advance my work in the Congress and inspire

volunteers during campaign seasons. In my last election, I faced a twenty-eight-year-old who boasted that he would crush me with the youth vote. That never materialized—we won among all demographics, including the youth vote. We got there first and connected with Millennials with a message and record that was optimistic and focused on improving the lives of all Americans. Data shows that Millennials generally choose libertarian over statist, control-based solutions. Despite that, the Democratic Party expects to get the youth vote and often takes it for granted. Republicans often write off that vote, which is a big mistake. We can win this demographic, but showing up matters. We have to reach out and explain our ideas and solutions to Millennials— and then *ask for their vote.*

This photo was taken following a Q&A session with students at Canajoharie Middle School in 2013.

A Message to Liberals

If you are a liberal and you've read this far, you must be commended. I hope to meet you in person someday, if I haven't already. I have a simple message for you: Come home to your roots. Leave the statist, Hegelian progressive movement that threatens this exceptional way of life and the values you hold dear. In my travels to places like Woodstock, New Paltz, and New York City, I have listened to your views and feel as if I understand your dreams and desires. At your core, you seek many of the same goals conservatives desire. You want freedom, security, sustainability, equal opportunity, and social justice. These are noble goals and areas where we agree. Candidly and sincerely, you have a much better chance of realizing them by helping me reform the Republican Party than staying with the decadent Democratic Party.

At the core of today's Democratic Party are two fundamental goals—the pursuit of economic justice and the pursuit of social justice. Both are worthy objectives, but the way the Democratic Party goes about advancing them causes epic failure for those who need the help most of all—those on the lower end of the socioeconomic spectrum. That is because they rely principally on "tax, borrow, and spend" economic approaches and on an expansive role for the federal government in every facet of American life. The central problem with this state-centered approach is that *it doesn't work.*

Nearly every place where Democratic policies dominate, we see failing local governments and imperiled people. When you get on the "tax, borrow, and spend" overnight bus, you're not sure why or how, but when you wake up, you end up in places like Detroit or Baltimore. There's got to be more to promoting economic success than just printing and spending money. If that were so, then Kazakhstan would just print $10 trillion and economically bury us. It doesn't work that way. We must produce value added in the economy, and for that we need the private sector to flourish. Democratic Party policies tend to be antigrowth, holding back the economy, which ultimately hurts working-class Americans looking for work or in pursuit of higher wages.

The Democratic Party rightly pursues social justice, but their approach is often one of "control," favoring policies that centralize and consolidate power in the federal government, specifically the office of the presidency and the bureaucracy. The premise comes straight out of the playbook of nineteenth-century German idealism, where the all-powerful state will perfect man. That will never happen—nor should it. American founding principles, while not without fault, work best because they are most closely aligned with human nature. We are different from Europe and the rest of the world by choice. Humans strongly desire freedom and security, so they anticipate a role for government—they just don't want it in every facet of life. We have seen the failures of big government— approaches that lack efficacy. Bureaucrats in Washington, D.C., however well intentioned, simply don't know better than local offi cials, volunteers in not-for-profit and faith-based organizations, and entrepreneurs in our communities.

In the battle of ideas, the Democratic Party is losing. Big government not only is ineffective, it is also easily corrupted. Today we have bloated government and a rigged system that responds to moneyed interests. We desperately need reform, but the answer is not to expand government and give it more control. Like the economy in the information age, we need to streamline government and decentralize power.

The best way for liberals to achieve their heart's desire is to reject statist policies and embrace founding principles that support economic freedom and balance that with societal norms that inspire us to fulfill our obligations to family and friends through works of charity in our communities. National policies should be focused on securing liberty and justice for all and facilitating prosperity, sustainability, and equal opportunity. Social justice is best pursued at the local level, through volunteerism and not-for-profit organizations.

It would drive my political opposition crazy, but the economically poorest areas in my district voted for me with the largest margins. Partisan Democrats thought that was insane, believing these people were voting against their own interest. They were *not* voting against their interests. They knew exactly what they were doing. They don't want handouts. They want *opportunity*, and they see very well what "tax, borrow, and spend" policies do to their local economies and workers' wages and how "control" policies adversely impact their freedom. They don't want to be trapped in perpetual welfare with no hope. They want upward mobility and freedom.

This plays out in national elections, too. In the 2016 presidential campaign, the so-called "blue wall" of working-class states (Pennsylvania, Ohio, Michigan, and Wisconsin) flipped to vote for Donald Trump. With wages stuck at 1999 levels and jobs leaving for overseas destinations, voters wanted change—to "drain the swamp." In that political environment, what did the Democrats offer? A candidate who was paid hundreds of thousands of dollars for twenty-minute speeches on Wall Street and offered economic proposals with more of the same, where the delicate balance between workers' interests and environmental protection was scrapped with primacy to the latter. Like liberty and security, working-class people ask, "Why can't we have both economic opportunity and environmental conservation?"

The answer is, you can—but you need to vote for it.

There is a difference between motion and movement. Progressives put a premium on motion. If the national government is doing things, life is better for people. That's not always the case. Some government action is harmful. We should focus on movement toward better outcomes for people, rather than governmental motion. A reformed Republican Party is best to achieve economic and social justice.

Team Gibson

Over the course of the six years I served in Congress, our team's political strength continued to increase, despite a significant change in our district boundary that brought roughly four hundred thousand new constituents in 2013, when it was redrawn as the 19th after redistricting. This was a huge challenge. After redistricting, approximately 60 percent of our district was new. Going through that experience, I sometimes joked that I got to run for Congress for the first time twice.

By staying true to those voters who first sent me to Congress, while constantly reaching out to new voters, I was able to make significant inroads into the traditional Democratic base. The results were clear and stunning. In 2014, despite my being outspent more than two to one in a Democratic-leaning district that President Obama carried by over six points in 2012, I won reelection by nearly 30 percent. Further, my favorable/unfavorable rating in the summer of 2016, as I was wrapping up my time in Congress, was 86 percent to 7 percent among registered Republicans and 60 percent to 30 percent among registered Democrats, something the independent pollster stated was completely unheard of in a competitive district in these especially divisive times.

Much of the credit goes to our hardworking and dedicated team. I surrounded myself with strong women, starting at home with Mary Jo and our two daughters, Katie and Maggie. At work,

I had exceptional staff leadership, including my chief of staff, Stephanie Valle, my deputy chief of staff, Rebecca Shaw, my executive assistant, Kate Better, and our deputy district director, Ann Mueller. With over 53 percent of the electorate composed of women, I never lacked for insights and advice on the female voter, because I had to win over and keep the support of my inner circle every day.

Moreover, we had a staff that looked like America, allowing us to reach out and connect with all people. George Christian, a black American and retired Army veteran, ran my office in Kingston, the largest city in my district. George is a charismatic people person who was widely known in Kingston, throughout Ulster County, and beyond. Kingston also has a large Hispanic community, and having a fluent Spanish speaker on staff, Corinne Boughton, was very helpful. While Corinne eventually moved on to take a higher-paying job in the private sector, she helped us make connections in the Hispanic community that George was able to sustain for our entire period of service. We also hired a large number of veterans. At one point over 33 percent of our paid staff had veteran status, and combined with our veteran volunteers, who numbered in the hundreds, they enabled us to connect with large numbers of constituents—veterans comprise over 15 percent of the district. We also had on staff a former village mayor, the clerk of a county legislature, and a successful small business owner. All three of these women were popular and well-connected in their communities. Without their incredible work and the dedication of the entire staff, we wouldn't have been able to achieve these remarkable results.

With this team and these methods, over time, we were able to unify and grow our political support, and in Congress that translated into meaningful results for our district. Using a similar approach, we can take this nationwide.

Conclusion

The Lessons of the 2016 Presidential Campaign

This past presidential election cycle was truly unprecedented. For the first time ever, we had a presidential nominee with absolutely no government experience. Previously, candidates had either some governmental or military service, or both. Also, for the first time ever, a woman was the nominee of a major political party. We also broke ground in a bad way when for the first time ever, both political candidates went into election day with unfavorable ratings above 50 percent.

Some have also described it as the most vitriolic campaign in history, although I question the claim. Read *Magnificent Catastrophe* and see that the 1800 presidential election between John Adams and Thomas Jefferson was vicious. Still, I agree with the larger point: In the modern age we've never witnessed such a personally negative campaign, with neither candidate offering a compelling positive vision for the future.

Despite all this, elections occur, and afterward, someone wins and someone loses. Donald Trump is now president of the United States. Three words explain his victory: jobs, wages, and reform. Trump promised the American people he would deliver more of all three. He deserves a chance to follow through on his campaign pledges. At the same time, he should be held accountable for these promises, as they are exactly what the country needs right now. I didn't vote for Donald Trump in the primary and have very mixed views about him even now, mostly unfavorable. We had horrific choices in the general election, but I did not dodge my responsibility. I voted for Trump because he was the only candidate who could bring the change we need—jobs, wages, and reform. His opponent, Hillary Clinton, would have been more of the same—"peace through weakness," economic decline, and corruption.

With Trump's victory, Democrats are now in disarray, trying to figure out what went wrong and how to fix it. Republicans are ascendant, now empowered with unified government in Washington. However, both political parties should be careful about drawing hasty conclusions in the aftermath. It was a complex election, with issues, personalities, and trends cutting in different directions.

Beyond jobs, wages, and reform, here are my significant takeaways from this election:

1. Relying primarily on discrediting your opponent is not good strategy. Hillary Clinton throughout, but particularly in the end, closed with the argument that you simply can't elect Donald Trump, so, sorry—like it or not, I'm your next president. That didn't work.
2. The American people are increasingly rejecting the statist policies of the Democratic Party.
3. Regarding points 1 and 2, many national leaders in the Democratic Party have not gotten the message.
4. Republican voters are rejecting the neoconservative positions that have held sway in their party since the 9/11 attacks. These neoconservative views are increasingly labeled as

"establishment" and "globalist," neither of which attract much support among base Republican voters.

5. Even though many Trump voters held an unfavorable view of him, he was the "change" candidate on the ballot, and thus many Americans voted for him. Trump's platform was real and the Republican Party must change.

6. Regarding points 4 and 5, many national leaders in the Republican Party have not gotten the message.

7. Voters are disgusted with politics. Polling throughout the campaign consistently showed that the majority of voters disliked both major candidates and wanted a new direction for the country.

8. Some believe that the message of this election is that the country wants non–politically correct so-called alpha males to run this country, even at the expense of founding principles that limit power. Expect this to spawn Trump-like candidates across all levels of government, in both political parties.

9. Point 8 is a mistake. Americans are good-natured people who believe in the Golden Rule and founding principles. Although without question we were in need of a course correction, having gone overboard with political correctness in recent years, historically the American people follow leaders who inspire the best in us and who treat people with dignity and respect. Americans believe in founding principles and our exceptional way of life and ultimately will not give that up for authoritarian approaches.

10. Point 9 should *not* be construed to mean Trump's agenda was wrong. Trump's agenda was largely effective and resonating (minus the unconstitutional positions advocating religious tests, torture, and circumscribing the First Amendment).

11. The philosophy and positions presented in this book will unify and grow the conservative movement and rally the American people around founding principles that will strengthen the republic and revitalize the American dream.

The Party of Lincoln

We are now off and running in 2017. The Trump administration has put up some wins and has suffered some significant setbacks. It's still hard to see where this is all going. It's not especially surprising. We hired a guy without a strong set of principles and beliefs. While he articulated an agenda that connected with the American people, President Trump lacks the core strength of deeply held views. Once his agenda makes contact with Washington, D.C., and challenges present themselves, President Trump quickly lashes out and often pivots, confusing his supporters and weakening his efforts. Ironically, for a person lauded for his dominating style, he lacks the mental toughness to see through hard tasks, largely because he is not fully committed to them in the first place. Still, as a disrupter and agent of change, we are better off with Trump than Clinton, although we're likely in for more turbulence in the months and years to come.

In these challenging times, the GOP can draw inspiration from its first president—Abraham Lincoln. Lincoln possessed remarkable moral and physical courage and led this country in its darkest times, when the very existence of the Union weighed in the balance. In the summer of 1864, he was at his nadir of support. In Washington, there was talk of potentially convening a second nominating convention so that Lincoln could be dropped from the Republican ticket. Such an action would have been unprecedented. Given his flagging support, in late August, President Lincoln seriously considered sending a letter to Confederate president Jefferson Davis inquiring about terms for peace. He even drafted a letter to that effect, only to tear it up the next day.

Sometimes dire situations can turn around overnight in unexpected ways. In early September, the Union army captured Atlanta. That victory electrified the North and carried Lincoln to political victory in the election that November over his former commanding general, George McClellan, who promised an immediate, honorable end to the war. Imagine what would have happened if things had turned out differently.

The nation is fortunate that President Lincoln possessed the moral courage to stick to his convictions. A lesser man would have crumbled under such pressure, ending the war prematurely and leaving the stain of slavery intact for at least another generation, with the specter of more bloodshed still in front of us. We were saved from that fate because of exceptional, principled leadership.

President Lincoln was also personally fearless. He stood six feet four inches tall, still today the tallest president in our history. That height was especially unusual in the 1860s and would be the equivalent of six foot ten or so today. Lincoln stood above most others and was widely recognized, yet within a couple of days of Richmond falling to the Union in April 1865, he walked through the streets of that city. The residents immediately identified him and were shocked that he would take that much risk to walk among them. Lincoln was a clear target for any angry Confederate looking to make history with an assassin's bullet. The president considered the danger but knew how important his personal leadership was to calming and reassuring the people of Richmond that our nation would come together and heal. That powerful leadership should inspire us now. We are still the Party of Lincoln.

I'm offering this book to help us rally in these challenging times. We should not "cut and run" from many of the populist ideas advanced in the 2016 campaign. The swamp must be drained. We need significant political reform to restore faith in our ability to be self-governing. To rally the American people and effect change, we need leadership that helps people see the connections between original founding principles, where we have strayed, and what needs to be done to get back on track. In that process, we want to be united and inspired, not divided and commanded by an authoritarian leader with a caustic and demeaning style.

Let's keep faith in our exceptional way of life and renew the spirit of Philadelphia. Going forward, let's empower the right people who are prepared to lead. We need leaders of character, who inspire others and treat people right, and drive us to advance the cause of freedom. We need leaders who do not lose heart, do not become distracted or nasty at the first sign of danger. Anyone can be gracious in the good times. The real test of character is how you handle adversity and challenge—that's when real leaders focus and get things done. They are out there. Keep faith. Let's get this done.

Acknowledgments

This book would not have been possible without the significant help of many others. First, I thank Sean Desmond, my editor at Twelve, who provided sage advice on how to organize and frame the book and significantly improved my ability to communicate the main points. The entire team at Twelve was great to work with, and I thank them all, especially Rachel Kambury, Roland Ottewell, Carolyn Kurek, Paul Samuelson, and Brian McLendon.

Along the way, many folks provided ideas and read drafts of the book, including Dan Allyn, George Will, Ed Meese, Stephanie Valle, Rebecca Shaw, Bob Gibson, Brad Gentile, Steve Bulger, Ann Mueller, George Christian, Nick Czajka, Paula Brown, Patty Hohmann, James McAllister, Todd Young, Elise Stefanik, Chris Stewart, Dan Lipinski, Mike Bittel, George Gerardi, Mary Howard, and Bob Oster. I thank them all for their friendship and support.

It was a great privilege to serve the people of upstate New York in the Congress. For all the frustrations and disappointments, I never lost sight of the fact that this is still a great country filled with tremendous people, and our form of government, for all its faults, is still superior to any other out there. I'll be forever grateful to my constituents for giving me the privilege of serving them and to my hardworking staff, who made a positive difference every day. Mary Jo and I are very thankful for all the friends we've made along the way. My colleagues in Congress are often maligned, but they are in the main honorable and good folks doing their best to serve this great nation. I miss them already. I especially thank the New York delegation. I enjoyed our periodic gatherings to deliberate on the issues and the other times we got together just to enjoy each other's company.

In many ways, this book is autobiographical, and I'm deeply grateful for all the love and support I've had throughout my entire life beginning with my parents, Bob and Barbara Gibson, and my siblings, Kathleen, Bob, and Tim and their families—and to our entire extended Gibson and Gerardi families. And to my lifelong friends, Mark Zander and Doug Stoliker—it's wonderful to now have more time to spend together. As I reflect on my upbringing, I must express gratitude to my teachers. I learned a great deal from them and especially thank them for their encouragement.

For twenty-nine years, I served in the U.S. military, and apart from family, these experiences and relationships have most shaped who I am today. I was incredibly fortunate to serve alongside so many great Americans. I'm grateful for your friendship and support and acknowledge the many sacrifices by service members and their families in the cause of protecting this exceptional way of life. I greatly appreciated all of the soldiers I served with, beginning with my time in the New York Army National Guard. Having served three tours in the 82nd Airborne Division, I'd be remiss if I didn't single out my former paratroopers and their families, especially the Falcons. I will always remember your remarkable courage, dedication, and skill and constantly think of those we lost, including Zach Wobler and Chris Pusateri, to whom this book is dedicated—we are forever grateful. And as with my teachers, I also thank my former bosses in the Army who helped develop and mentor me over the years, especially John Davis, Brian Joyce, Larry White, Glenn Marsh, Paul Trotti,

Abe Turner, Jim Golden, Dan Kaufman, Rob Gordon, Mike Meese, Don Snider, Jim Klingaman, Bernie Champoux, Bryan Stephens, Kurt Fuller, Jeff Bailey, Gary Patton, Jeff Eckstein, Mick Bednarek, Craig Nixon, Randy Mixon, H. R. McMaster, Mark Milley, Bob Brown, Bill Caldwell, David Rodriguez, Curt Scaparrotti, Bruce Scott, and Dan Allyn. Each of them made a lasting impact on my life, and I'm grateful. While in the Army I had one-year assignments with the office of Congressman Jerry Lewis and the Hoover Institution at Stanford University. Mary Jo and I made wonderful friendships during those experiences and we cherish those memories and relationships. Recently, Hoover invited me back as a member of the Role of Military History in Contemporary Conflict Working Group. I look forward to the new challenges ahead.

I now have the good fortune of also serving on the faculty at Williams College. The transition has been outstanding, and I appreciate the opportunity to teach and mentor such talented young folks. The students are awesome. I thank Justin Crowe and James McAllister for reaching out to recruit me for this new and exciting phase in my life.

Finally, I thank my family. Mary Jo is the most incredible person in the world: a loving wife, supermom, devoted daughter and sibling, supportive friend to so many, and a dedicated professional—a licensed clinical social worker helping veterans with PTSD and other life challenges. I'm the luckiest man on earth. Together, we love our children, Katie, Maggie, and Connor, and wish the best for them in their lives. It's wonderful to be able to share this journey with them. Amen.

Notes

Introduction

For polling data on the 2016 presidential election, I used the website RealClearPolitics (http://www.realclearpolitics.com/), which compiles polling data from a multitude of sources and research institutions.

On American exceptionalism, I consulted Seymour Martin Lipset, *American Exceptionalism: A Double-Edged Sword* (New York: Norton, 1996), and Louis Hartz, *The Liberal Tradition in America* (New York: Harcourt, Brace & World, 1955).

For more on the founding era, see Bernard Bailyn, *The Ideological Origins of the American Revolution* (Boston: Harvard University Press, 1967), and Daniel Boorstin, *The Genius of American Politics* (Chicago: University of Chicago Press, 1953). These works were influential in developing my thinking on the topic.

Chapter 1: Practice Peace through Strength

For more on my battalion's experiences in Iraq, see Christopher P. Gibson, "Battlefield Victories and Strategic Success," *Military Review* (October–November 2006): 47–59. To read more about Sergeant Chris Pusateri and Staff Sergeant Zachary Wobler, see the website Honor the Fallen (thefallen.militarytimes.com).

Regarding the "social contract," I am indebted to a series of classics in philosophy, including Thomas Hobbes, *Leviathan* (New York: Penguin, 1984; originally published in 1651), John Locke, *Second Treatise of Government* (New York: Cambridge University Press, 1994; originally published in 1689), Jean-Jacques Rousseau, *The Social Contract* (1762), Edmund Burke, "Speech to the Electors at Bristol at the Conclusion of the Poll" (1774), and Charles-Louis Montesquieu, *The Spirit of the Laws* (Kitchener, ON: Batoche, 2001; originally published in 1748).

For more on my critique of neoconservatism, see Christopher P. Gibson, *Securing the State: Reforming the National Security Decisionmaking Process at the Civil-Military Nexus* (Burlington, VT: Ashgate Press, 2008). On the rise of neoconservatism, see James Mann, *The Rise of the Vulcans: The History of Bush's War Cabinet* (New York: Viking, 2004).

There is no shortage of insightful works on President Ronald Reagan. My favorite is Craig Shirley, *Rendezvous with Destiny: Ronald Reagan and the Campaign That Changed America* (Wilmington, DE: ISI Books, 2009). See also H. W. Brands, *Reagan: The Life* (New York: Doubleday, 2015). For a detailed policy discussion, see Charles O. Jones, ed., *The Reagan Legacy: Promise and Performance* (Chatham, NJ: Chatham House, 1988).

For more on deterrence, see Thomas Schelling, *The Strategy of Conflict* (Boston: Harvard University Press, 1980 reprint), Bernard Brodie, *Strategy in the Missile Age* (Princeton, NJ: Princeton University Press, 1959), Stephen Walt, *The Origins of Alliances* (Ithaca, NY: Cornell University Press, 1987), Kenneth Walz, *Theory of International Politics* (New York: McGraw-Hill, 1979), and John Mearsheimer, *Conventional Deterrence* (Ithaca, NY: Cornell University Press, 1983). All of these works influenced my thought on the subject.

Sun Tzu is still a must-read for all serious students of strategy. See Sun Tzu, *The Art of War* (Minneapolis: Filiquarian, 2007). With regard to major threats we face today, I consulted Anthony Cordesman, "The Imploding US Strategy in the Islamic State War?," Center for Strategic and International Studies, October 23, 2014; Ilan Goldenberg, Nicholas Heras, and Paul Scharre, "Defeating the Islamic State," Center for a New American Security, June 16, 2016; Christopher K. Johnson, "President Xi Jinping's 'Belt and Road' Initiative," Center for Strategic and International Studies, March 28, 2016; Michael S. Chase and Arthur Chan, "China's Evolving Approach to 'Integrated Strategic Deterrence,'" Rand Corporation, April 7, 2016; Paul K. Davis et al., "Deterrence and Stability for the Korean Peninsula," *Korean Journal of Defense Analysis* 28, no. 1 (March 2016): 1–23; Christopher S. Chivvis and Stephen J. Flanagan, "NATO's

Russia Problem: The Alliance's Tough Road Ahead Post–Warsaw Summit," *National Interest*, July 13, 2016; William Courtney and Martin C. Libicki, "How to Counter Putin's Subversive War on the West," *National Interest*, August 1, 2016; David Shlapak and Michael Johnson, "Reinforcing Deterrence on NATO's Eastern Flank: Wargaming the Defense of the Baltics," Rand Corporation, 2016; Kenneth Pollack, "US Policy toward the Middle East After the Iranian Nuclear Agreement," Brookings Institution, August 5, 2015; and Graham Fuller, *The "Center of the Universe": The Geopolitics of Iran* (Boulder, CO: Westview Press, 1991).

For more on the defense budget, visit the House Armed Services Committee website (https://armedservices.house.gov). See also Craig Whitlock, "Pentagon Buries Evidence of $125 Billion in Bureaucratic Waste," *Washington Post*, December 5, 2016.

The Weinberger-Powell Doctrine was unveiled by Secretary of Defense Caspar Weinberger on November 28, 1984, in a speech entitled, "The Uses of Military Power," National Press Club.

For more on fiscal year 2017 National Defense Authorization Act, visit https://armedservices.house.gov/hearings-and-legislation/ndaa-national -defense-authorization-act. For more on the future of the U.S. nuclear arsenal, see Michaela Dodge, "The Future of the U.S. Nuclear Program," Heritage Foundation, August 8, 2012, http://www.heritage.org /defense/report/the-future-the-us-nuclear-weapons-program. For more on the future of U.S. missile defense, see "The Future of U.S. Army Missile Defense," Center for Strategic and International Studies, https:// www.csis.org/events/future-us-army-missile-defense. You can learn more about the future of U.S. airpower at "Charting a Future for U.S. Air Power," Council on Foreign Relations, March 24, 2015, http://www .cfr.org/defense-and-security/charting-future-us-air-power/p36292. For an interesting take on the future of U.S. sea power, see Michael C. Horowitz, "Ensuring the Future of Naval Power Projection: The Role of Carrier Action," February 11, 2016, http://www.michaelchorowitz .com/Documents/HorowitzTestimony2-11-16.pdf.Regardinglandpower, read the Army's Operating Concept at https://www.pritzkermilitary .org/files/7814/5988/0225/The_Army_Operating_Concept_31_October .pdf. Also view Army lieutenant general H. R. McMaster's work at Pritzker

Military Museum & Library, https://www.pritzkermilitary.org/whats_on
/pritzker-military-presents/lt-general-hr-mcmaster-harbingers-future-war/.

For helping develop the Posture Act, I thank Army generals Dan Allyn
and H. R. McMaster and House Armed Services Committee professional
staff member John Wasson. Also for their diligent staff work I thank Nick
Czajka, Major Pat McGuigan, and Colonel Stephen Ledbetter.

For more on the development of AirLand Battle doctrine, see John
Romjue, *From Active Defense to AirLand Battle: The Development of Army
Doctrine, 1973–1982* (Fort Leavenworth, KS: Command and General
Staff College, 1984). For an informative account on the Persian Gulf
War, see Michael Gordon and Bernard Trainor, *The Generals' War: The
Inside Story of the Conflict in the Gulf* (Boston: Little, Brown, 1995).
For more on the 1994 U.S. showdown with Haiti, see Philippe Girard,
"Peacekeeping, Politics, and the 1994 US Intervention in Haiti," *Journal
of Conflict Studies* 24, no. 1 (2004). For more on Supreme Allied Com-
mander General Scaparrotti's views, see Lisa Ferdinando, "NATO Needs
'Position of Strength' for Russia," *DoD News*, September 18, 2016. I con-
sulted all of these works.

President George W. Bush's momentous speech at West Point graduation in 2002 may be read at "Text of Bush's Speech at West Point," *New
York Times*, June 1, 2002, http://www.nytimes.com/2002/06/01/inter
national/text-of-bushs-speech-at-west-point.html.

You can learn more about the combat actions of the 25th Infantry
Division (Tropic Lightning) during the Surge by visiting the website
maintained by the Institute for the Study of War: http://www.under
standingwar.org/operation/operation-lightning-hammer-i.

President Reagan's iconic speech at the Berlin War in June 1987
may be read at The History Place, http://www.historyplace.com/speeches
/reagan-tear-down.htm.

Chapter 2: Restore Founding Principles

There are many outstanding biographies for Benjamin Franklin. My
favorite is Walter Isaacson, *Benjamin Franklin: An American Life* (New
York: Simon & Schuster, 2004). See also Edmund Morgan, *Benjamin
Franklin* (New Haven, CT: Yale University Press, 2002), and H. W. Brands,

The First American: The Life and Times of Benjamin Franklin (New York: Anchor, 2010).

To read about the final poll taken before the election by the *New York Times* and CBS that found that 83 percent of respondents were disgusted with the 2016 presidential race, see Jonathan Martin, Dalia Sussman, and Megan Thee-Brenan, "Voters Express Disgust over U.S. Politics in New Times/CBS Poll," *New York Times*, November 3, 2016, https://www.nytimes.com/2016/11/04/us/politics/hillary-clinton-donald-trump-poll.html?_r=0. For more on David Hume, see *Essays: Moral, Political and Literary* (Indianapolis: Liberty Fund, 1987). You can learn more about the eighth president of the United States, Martin Van Buren, and my small village in upstate New York by visiting the National Park Service's page on his National Historic Site at https://www.nps.gov/mava/index.htm. The website for American University's Washington Semester Program is http://www.american.edu/spexs/washingtonsemester/. Congressman John Faso's website is https://faso.house.gov/. For more on the Hoover Institution National Security Affairs Fellows Program, see http://www.hoover.org/fellows/category/national-security-affairs-fellows.

For more on the French Revolution, see George Lefebvre, *The Coming of the French Revolution* (Princeton, NJ: Princeton University Press, 1947). In this chapter I also drew insights from Arthur Herman, *The Cave and the Light: Plato Versus Aristotle and the Struggle for the Soul of Western Civilization* (New York: Random House, 2013), and from the previously cited works by Hobbes, Locke, Rousseau, and Montesquieu. Three other important works that influenced my thinking include Alexis de Tocqueville, *Democracy in America* (New York: Penguin Classics, 2013; originally published in two volumes in 1835 and 1840), Robert Bellah et al., *Habits of the Heart: Individualism and Commitment in American Life* (Berkeley: University of California Press, 1985), and Georg Wilhelm Friedrich Hegel, *Elements of the Philosophy of Right* (Cambridge: Cambridge University Press, 1991; originally published in 1820). Documents cited throughout that are accessible via the Internet include the Declaration of Independence, Articles of Confederation, U.S. Constitution, and Bill of Rights. A very interesting and informative book that impacted my thinking and that I subsequently shared with my constituents was Edward

Larson, *Magnificent Catastrophe: The Tumultuous Election of 1800, America's First Presidential Campaign* (New York: Free Press, 2007). See also Isaac Kramnick, ed., *The Federalist Papers* (Gloucester, MA: Peter Smith Publishing, 1987). Louis Hartz's previously cited work was also consulted for this chapter.

I strongly recommend David Brooks, *The Road to Character* (New York: Random House Books, 2015), which influenced my thinking.

For more on the 1947 National Security Act, see Douglas T. Stuart, *Creating the National Security State: A History of the Law that Transformed America* (Princeton, NJ: Princeton University Press, 2009). NSC 68 is now declassified and can be viewed online at https://publicintelligence .net/nsc-68/.

For more on former president Lyndon B. Johnson, see Robert Caro's renowned series published by Alfred A. Knopf that includes *The Path to Power* (1982), *Means of Ascent* (1990), *Master of the Senate* (2002), and *The Passage of Power* (2012). For more on the Patriot Act, see Cary Stacy Smith and Li-Ching Hung, *The Patriot Act: Issues and Controversies* (Springfield, IL: Charles C. Thomas, 2010).

For this chapter I also consulted James F. Simon, *FDR and Chief Justice Hughes: The President, the Supreme Court, and the Epic Battle over the New Deal* (New York: Simon & Schuster, 2012), Richard Hofstadter, *The Age of Reform* (New York: Vintage Books, 1955), Stephen E. Ambrose, *Nixon*, vol. 2, *The Triumph of a Politician, 1962–1972* (New York: Simon & Schuster, 1989), Michael J. Hillyard, *Cincinnatus and the Citizen-Servant Ideal: The Roman Legend's Life, Times, and Legacy* (Bloomington, IN: Xlibris, 2001), Zephyr Teachout, *Corruption in America: From Benjamin Franklin's Snuff Box to Citizens United* (Cambridge, MA: Harvard University Press, 2016), and Richard Kohn, *Eagle and Sword: The Federalists and the Creation of the Military Establishment in America, 1783–1802* (New York: Free Press, 1975).

My bill the War Powers Reform Act may be viewed at https://www .congress.gov/bill/113th-congress/house-bill/383. A media story about my proposal to my Democratic challenger to self-impose campaign finance limits during the 2014 election cycle is John Mason, "Gibson Challenges Eldridge to $2M Spending Limit," *Register-Star* (Hudson,

NY), April 16, 2014, http://www.registerstar.com/news/article_cd34289e
-c51e-11e3-99ec-001a4bcf887a.html.

Chapter 3: Promote a Flourishing Life

I thank Dr. Daniel Robinson, Distinguished Professor of Philosophy at Georgetown University, for first bringing my attention to the significance of eudaimonia. For more on self-actualization, see Abraham Maslow, "A Theory of Human Motivation," *Psychological Review* 50 (1943): 370–96.

On Dr. Martin Luther King, see "Letter from the Birmingham Jail," at http://www.africa.upenn.edu/Articles_Gen/Letter_Birmingham.html; "I Have a Dream" at http://www.americanrhetoric.com/speeches/mlki haveadream.htm; and Michael Honey, ed., *"All Labor Has Dignity"* (Boston: Beacon, 2012). These works were consulted for this chapter.

For more on farm regulations, see "Concentrated Animal Feeding Operations," U.S. Government Accountability Office, http://www.gao .gov/products/GAO-08-944. For more on milk prices and dairy payments, see Mark Stephenson, "Understand Your Milk Check," *Dairy Herd*, January 17, 2011, http://www.dairyherd.com/dairy-herd/features/understand -your-milk-check-113988639.html, and Daily Dairy Report, http://www .dailydairyreport.com/. You can read the federal farm bill enacted during the 113th Congress at https://www.gpo.gov/fdsys/pkg/BILLS-113hr2642enr /pdf/BILLS-113hr2642enr.pdf. The full text of the Trans-Pacific Partnership (TPP) trade agreement is available at https://ustr.gov/trade-agreements /free-trade-agreements/trans-pacific-partnership/TPP-Full-Text. My bill to reform agricultural labor may be viewed at https://www.congress.gov /bill/114th-congress/house-bill/1805. For more on upstate New York as the breadbasket of the American Revolution, see "Montgomery Place: An American Arcadia," http://american-arcadia.hudsonvalley.org/content/agriculture -intro3. To view the Beginning Farmer and Rancher Opportunity Act of 2013, see https://www.congress.gov/bill/113th-congress/house-bill/1727 /text. A media story covering my advocacy for the Beginning Farmer and Rancher Opportunity Act is John Mason, "Gibson Promotes Young Farmers," *Register-Star* (Hudson, NY) April 23, 2013, http://www.registerstar .com/news/article_534eb542-abcc-11e2-89d2-0019bb2963f4.html. You can view video footage from "dairy boot camp" at "Congressman Gibson on the Farm," YouTube, https://www.youtube.com/watch?v=A_uCifwh-A8.

News coverage of one of my visits to Amphenol can be viewed at Denise Richardson, "Lawmakers Take Virtual Ride at Amphenol," *Daily Star* (Oneonta, NY), September 26, 2014, http://www.thedailystar.com/news /local_news/lawmakers-take-virtual-ride-at-amphenol/article_d1ffebc6 -c07d-524d-8e79-6106347ed857.html. For more on the Skills Act, see http://edworkforce.house.gov/skillsact/. You can learn more about Ioxus at http://ioxus.com/english/. The paper cited in this chapter is the *Hometown Oneonta*, whose publisher is Jim Kevlin of Cooperstown. The website for the Otsego County Chamber of Commerce is http://otsegocc.com/.

You can view the Partnership to Build America Act of 2013 at https:// www.congress.gov/bill/113th-congress/house-bill/2084/text. The Brown-fields Redevelopment Tax Incentive Authorization Act of 2014 can be viewed at https://www.congress.gov/bill/113th-congress/house-bill/4542/text?q=% 7B%22search%22%3A%5B%22Gibson+Esty+Brownfield%22%5D%7 D&r=1. You can learn more about Schmidt's Wholesale of Monticello, New York, at http://www.schmidtswholesale.com/. Regarding 21st Century Cures and the Lyme Bill, you can learn more at "New Lyme Language in Con-gress's 21st Century Cures Bill," LymeDisease.org, November 29, 2016, https://www.lymedisease.org/new-lyme-language-congresss-21st-century -cures-bill/. You can read the text of the Every Student Succeeds Act at https:// www.congress.gov/bill/114th-congress/senate-bill/1177. To learn more about the 1996 Welfare Reform Act, see http://royce.house.gov/uploadedfiles/the %201996%20welfare%20reform%20law.pdf. You can view analysis of the Cooper-LaTourette bipartisan budget at Shai Akabas and Loren Adler, "Cooper-LaTourette Fiscal Year 2013 Budget: The Details," Bipartisan Policy Center, March 29, 2012, http://bipartisanpolicy.org/blog/cooper-latourette -fiscal-year-2013-budget-details/. You can learn more about Medicare Advantage at https://www.medicare.gov/sign-up-change-plans/medicare -health-plans/medicare-advantage-plans/medicare-advantage-plans.html.

Chapter 4: Keep Faith

To learn about Tug McGraw and the 1973 New York Mets, see Rich Klein, "Ya Gotta Believe: Tug and the 1973 New York Mets," *Sports Col-*

lectors Daily, March 17, 2014, http://www.sportscollectorsdaily.com
/ya-gotta-believe-tug-1973-new-york-mets/. The previously cited work
by Arthur Herman (*The Cave and the Light*) influenced my thinking for
this chapter. I also consulted with three works by Aristotle (*Metaphys-
ics*, *Nicomachean Ethics*, and *Politics*); Plato's *Republic*; Ronald Reagan's
speeches "Election Eve Address 'A Vision for America,'" November 3,
1980, American Presidency Project, http://www.presidency.ucsb.edu
/ws/?pid=85199, and "Inaugural Address," January 20, 1981, ibid., http://
www.presidency.ucsb.edu/ws/?pid=43130; *The Autobiography of Benjamin Franklin*; and Friedrich Nietzsche's *Thus Spoke Zarathustra*.

You can learn more about my experiences in Iraq by viewing the previously cited work "Battlefield Victories and Strategic Success" that I published in *Military Review* in October 2006. You can learn more about the
"Out of the Darkness" walks at http://www.twcnews.com/nys/hudson
-valley/news/2015/09/13/suicide-prevention-walk-.html.

Chapter 5: Unify and Grow

The *New York Times* article referenced at the beginning of the chap-
ter is Michael Barbaro, "G.O.P. Representative in Upstate New York Is
Strong among Democrats," October 30, 2014, https://www.nytimes
.com/2014/10/31/nyregion/republican-congressman-in-an-upstate
-district-is-strong-among-democrats.html?_r=0. My favorite book on
Senator John McCain is Robert Timberg, *The Nightingale's Song* (New
York: Simon & Schuster, 1995). You can read an account of the 2010
Gibson-Murphy debate in Queensbury, New York, in Jimmy Velkind,
"Murphy Draws Boos at Forum," *Albany Times Union*, October 20,
2010, http://www.timesunion.com/local/article/Murphy-draws-boos-at
-forum-714444.php.

You can read more about the confusion over philosophical label-
ing in Zane McMillin, "Rep. Justin Amash 'Most Liberal Republican,'
GOP Strategist Karl Rove Says," Mlive.com, July 8, 2013, http://www
.mlive.com/news/grand-rapids/index.ssf/2013/07/rep_justin_amash
_most_liberal.html. You can learn more about actor Gary Sinise's effort
to help veteran Joe Wilkinson at https://www.garysinisefoundation.org
/events/joseph-wilkinson-benefit-concert.

For this chapter, I consulted Tip O'Neill, *All Politics Is Local* (New York: Time Books, 1994), and Neil Howe and William Strauss, *Millennials Rising: The Next Great Generation* (New York: Vintage, 2000).

For more on Congresswoman Elise Stefanik, see https://stefanik.house .gov/.

You can read more about the tribute I gave to my staff from the floor of the U.S. House at https://www.congress.gov/congressional-record /2016/7/14/house-section/article/h4989-3?r=9.

To view the results of the Siena Research Institute poll conducted in June 2016, see https://www.siena.edu/news-events/article/faso-republican -teachout-democrat-hold-large-double-digit-leads-in-their-re.

Conclusion

For the opening section, I consulted with the RealClearPolitics website for all polling data and election results, and Larson's *Magnificent Catastrophe*, previously cited.

For the section on President Lincoln, I consulted Stephen B. Oates, *With Malice toward None: A Life of Abraham Lincoln* (New York: Harper Perennial; reprint, 2011), and Bill O'Reilly and Martin Dugard, *Killing Lincoln: The Shocking Assassination That Changed America Forever* (New York: Henry Holt, 2011).

About the Author

Chris Gibson grew up in a working-class family in upstate New York, in the village of Kinderhook. The son of a union man, Chris attended Ichabod Crane public schools and was the point guard and co-captain of the high school basketball team.

At seventeen, Chris enlisted in the New York National Guard and later earned an ROTC commission at nearby Siena College. The first in his family to go to college, Chris graduated magna cum laude with a BA in history. He later earned an MPA, MA, and PhD in government from Cornell University and is the author of *Securing the State*, a book on national security decision making published in 2008.

After serving five years in the Army National Guard, Chris went on to serve twenty-four years in the U.S. Army, rising to the rank of colonel and deploying seven times. This included four combat tours to Iraq and separate deployments to Kosovo, the southwestern United States for a counterdrug operation, and, just prior to his retirement, Haiti, where he commanded the 82nd Airborne Division's 2nd Brigade Combat Team (BCT) during the opening month of a humanitarian relief operation. The secretary of the Army awarded the BCT the Superior Unit Award for their actions in Haiti.

Among Chris's military awards and decorations are two Legions of Merit, four Bronze Star Medals, the Purple Heart, the

Joint Service Commendation Medal, the Combat Infantryman's Badge with Star, the Master Parachutist Badge, and the Ranger Tab. For their actions in Mosul in support of the first national election in the new Iraq, his battalion task force earned the Valorous Unit Award. For their actions in Tal Afar during the second and third national elections in Iraq, his battalion and the 3rd Armored Cavalry Regiment were recognized for excellence by President George W. Bush and earned a second Valorous Unit Award.

Other key assignments included tours teaching American politics at the United States Military Academy at West Point, serving as a congressional fellow with U.S. Representative Jerry Lewis (R-CA), serving as the chairman of the Defense Appropriations Subcommittee, and completing a Hoover National Security Affairs Fellowship at Stanford University. Chris was also the distinguished honor graduate of the U.S. Army Command and General Staff College.

After retiring from the Army in 2010, Chris and his family returned home to Kinderhook. He was elected to Congress in November 2010 and served six years before self-imposing term limits and retiring. In Congress, Chris served on the House Armed Services, Agriculture, and Small Business Committees where he played an integral role in crafting national security, veterans, and agricultural policies and other significant legislation to grow the economy and advance constituent-driven issues.

Chris now serves as the Stanley Kaplan Visiting Professor of American Foreign Policy at Williams College, and as a member of the Hoover Institution's working group on the role of military history in contemporary conflict.

Chris has been married to Mary Jo, an NYS licensed clinical social worker who works for the Department of Veterans Affairs in Albany, for over twenty-one years, and they have three children: Katie (nineteen), Maggie (eighteen), and Connor (sixteen).

Mission Statement

Twelve strives to publish singular books by authors who have unique perspectives and compelling authority. Books that explain our culture; that illuminate, inspire, provoke, and entertain. Our mission is to provide a consummate publishing experience for our authors, one truly devoted to thoughtful partnership and cutting-edge promotional sophistication that reaches as many readers as possible. For readers, we aim to spark that rare reading experience—one that opens doors, transports, and possibly changes their outlook on our ever-changing world.

12 Things to Remember about TWELVE

1. Every Twelve book will enliven the national conversation.
2. Each book will be singular in voice, authority, or subject matter.
3. Each book will be carefully edited, designed, and produced.
4. Each book's publication life will begin with a monthlong launch; for that month it will be the imprint's devoted focus.
5. The Twelve team will work closely with its authors to devise a publication strategy that will reach as many readers as possible.

6. Each book will have a national publicity campaign devoted to reaching as many media outlets—and readers—as possible.
7. Each book will have a unique digital strategy.
8. Twelve is dedicated to finding innovative ways to market and promote its authors and their books.
9. Twelve offers true partnership with its authors—the kind of partnership that gives a book its best chance at success.
10. Each book will get the fullest attention and distribution of the sales force of the Hachette Book Group.
11. Each book will be promoted well past its on-sale date to maximize the life of its ideas.
12. Each book will matter.